MY MOLINE

MY
MOLINE

A
YOUNG
ILLEGAL
IMMIGRANT
DREAMS

by
John
Cervantes

Revised Edition

Published by the John R. Cervantes Memorial Scholarship Fund.
Visit JohnCervantes.org for more information.

Publisher's Cataloging-in-Publication Data

Names: Cervantes, John, author.
Title: My Moline / by John Cervantes.
Description: pp; cm.
Identifiers: LC PCN 2017913132 | ISBN 978-0-692-93883-6 (paperback)
Subjects: LCSH: Cervantes, John. | Mexican Americans—Illinois—
Moline—Biography. | Immigrants—United States—Biography. |
Mexicans—United States—Biography. | Illegal aliens—United States. |
Moline (Ill.)—Biography.
Classification: LCC F549.M7 C47 2017 | DDC 977.3/393—dc23

10 9 8 7 6 5 4 3 2

Author John Cervantes with the first edition of *My Moline*, 1986

FOREWORD

A cornerstone of the successful and fulfilling life of John Cervantes was his college education. As will be clear in this narrative, his college education was dependent on the help of a supportive Moline community, as well as financial assistance from Moline's Little Deere Chapter of the National Society Daughters of the American Revolution.

In honor of John Cervantes, who passed away in 2009, his family established the John R. Cervantes Memorial Scholarship, awarded each year to a deserving graduating senior of Moline High School. This scholarship is meant to assist these young scholars achieve their educational goals, while preserving the memory of John Cervantes.

The republishing of *My Moline*, which had previously been out of print for decades, is part of this effort. One hundred percent of the net proceeds from the sale of this revised edition go toward funding the scholarship named in the author's memory.

Readers are encouraged to donate directly to the fund as well. For more information about the scholarship fund, and how to donate, please visit JohnCervantes.org. More information about *My Moline*, including an interactive map of key places, is also available at the website.

Dedicated to the memory

of

Mary Josephine Holland,
Marjorie Adele Hendee,

and

All our other great teachers
who seldom see how far their
good influences reach.

MY MOLINE
A YOUNG ILLEGAL IMMIGRANT DREAMS

The true story of the events that lead a large Mexican family to flee the dangers of their homeland, and risk the uncertainties of illegal immigration into the United States.

After wandering from Texas to Montana, one branch of this family succeeds in establishing a permanent home in Moline, Illinois. Here the oldest boy finds a warm, nurturing environment that makes him feel like a real, proud, and happy American.

Nevertheless, his dreams of acquiring a college education are suddenly dimmed by his father's death, and his own status as an illegal immigrant. Fortunately, several Moliners encourage and support him wholeheartedly, confirming the author's belief that this land always was, and hopefully always will be, the land of opportunity for all who really strive to succeed.

TABLE OF CONTENTS

PREFACE

The original purpose of this book was to explain to my children (Ann, Elizabeth, Charles, Joseph, John Jr., Thomas, Mary, and Paul) why we had to make regular pilgrimages to Moline, Illinois. I could not simply explain to them that I considered Moline to be my spiritual home, because I could trace all of my sense of values to the many persons whose idealism had impinged on mine and molded those character traits within me which have served me well.

Of course, they could see that I returned to see my mother, brothers, sisters, nephews, nieces, and friends, but the City, itself, has continuously held a fascination for me that is a result of all I have written, and much more that I can't explain.

Undoubtedly, the scope of this writing has also been expanded by the kind reviews of all who have read the early manuscripts, including my high school literature teacher, Marjorie Adele Hendee, to whom I dedicate it in fond remembrance.

John R. Cervantes
May 1, 1986

ACKNOWLEDGMENTS

All of the persons mentioned in this book played a considerable part in my final decision to write it. Additionally, Maggie Peterson provided me with a small loft in her home during one of my many trips to Moline so that I could begin. Dolores Schatterman and Pamela Cervantes did the very first bit of typing for me. As I tried to rush the book to completion, my wife, Mildred, and my son-in-law, Jim Atkinson, spent many more hours typing and retyping. Jim, my daughter Mary, and my sister Mary Peterson were among my earliest supporters.

My sister-in-law, Margaret Cervantes, accompanied us when we first inquired into the cost and procedures for getting it printed. My son-in-law, David Kukla, has helped me prepare the manuscript for the printer. The line drawings were done by Jennifer Prager. I have received photographs from Jennie Taets, Leslie Swanson, Gus Flider, and my agent, Dorothy Johnson. She has been my staunchest supporter, and whenever I became disheartened she provided me with new ideas and inspiration.

I am truly thankful to all of these persons because without their help and encouragement, this book would not have been published.

John R. Cervantes
May 1, 1986

Family in Texas, circa 1920

Left to right, standing: Uncle Juan Trujillo, Dad; front row: Author, Mother, Aunt Cristina holding Author's brother, Tom

CHAPTER 1

ESCAPE

The fire sputtered and crackled inside the small wood burning stove. The yellowish-orange flames raced visibly across the bottom of the four lids and clawed up into the stove pipe where streaks could occasionally be seen shooting up past the damper as though determined to escape the radiant heat emanating along their hurried flight path.

Around the black stove, three small figures huddled close to each other trying to capture some of the heat with their extended hands. Once in a while, each would cross his arms and put his warm hands under his arm pits, hugging himself tightly as if to internalize the warmth. Whenever their faces got too warm, they would turn around with their backs to the stove in order to warm their behinds. Off to the side in an apple crate converted to a crib, a baby gurgled contentedly beneath his loose coverings of a baby blanket topped off by a small Mackinaw.

They were inside of a tar paper-covered shack with one large door in one corner and two small windows at the center and high up underneath the narrow eaves. The shack had been built as a farmer's tool shed. It was a long A-frame about 30 by 12 feet wide.

The studs and roof joists protruded nakedly into the interior. There were several nails partially driven into the studs about five feet from the rough plank wood flooring. These protruding nails were used as hooks for clothing, hats, belts, scarves, and even a couple of pots and pans. The floor had been set on top of stubby logs that leveled the floor about six inches from the frozen ground.

The wind whistled and moaned fiercely outside of the shack. Once in a while it would hurl a large tumbleweed or some other loose missile against its side. Just the day before, the farmer had stuffed straw all around the shack between the floor and the ground to keep the cold wind from coming up between the cracks in the floorboards.

He was hoping that the man and the woman he had hired to top his beets would not leave until the crop was safely in the sugar refinery. He felt sorry about their children because he had children of his own that he would never think of leaving unattended, but most of the other migrant workers had gone south to sunnier climate, and meanwhile this crop of sugar beets could make a great deal of difference in the amount of money his own family would have to tide them over until spring.

The four children inside the shack were all boys. The oldest one was 10 and the next one was six years old. Both of them should have been in school. Instead, they were watching their two-year-old brother and the small baby while their mother and father were away from daylight until dusk topping sugar beets.

All of them except the baby were uneasy. None of them could get used to the long day's absence by their parents. The oldest one could change the baby's diapers and mix his formula of Borden's milk and water. He could feed himself and the others whatever his mother had left in the pot for their lunch. He tried to hurry the passing of those long, lonely days by making up games and telling stories to his brothers, but he could not keep himself from feeling desolate. The responsibility of caring for his three brothers weighed heavily on his mind, and he could hardly wait for the return of his parents at the end of the day.

He noticed that the fire had started to die down, so he opened the lid to the fire box and crammed it full with some of the wood his father had brought in that morning. Within a couple of minutes, the fire roared into raging life. Sparks could be seen racing across the stove and upward into the chimney. What could not be seen was that one of these sparks was blown into the straw at the foot of the door and there it was immediately fanned into a consuming blaze.

The boys moved backward away from the hot stove. They heard a huffing, sucking sound, but it never occurred to any of them that the only doorway was then engulfed in flames until a gust of wind blew a cloud of smoke into the very area where they were still huddled around the stove.

The oldest boy quickly turned around and thought of escaping. He could see that the two windows were too small and too high. The smoke had continued to blow into the shack until his brothers began to cough with choking.

Without a word, he picked the baby out of his crib, threw the small Mackinaw over his face and shepherded the rest toward the flame-engulfed doorway.

The smoke and the acrid heat near the entrance was blinding and drove everyone back against the wall. At this point, the oldest boy yelled in desperation. "Hold someone's hand as tightly as you can and run right through the middle of the fire."

The two-year-old moved away from the fire toward the other end of the shack. The oldest boy then put the baby on the floor, chased his recalcitrant brother down, caught him, ran him toward the opening which was now getting larger and threw him right through the middle of the flames. Then he went back, picked up the baby, took his other brother by the hand and raced madly through the flames.

From the outside he could see that the whole quarter of the shack nearest to the door had now been consumed by the fire. He looked around at the rest of his brothers and noticed that they were frightened, bewildered, and shivering from the cold.

A team of horses pulling a flat wagon with a large round wooden barrel raced up to the scene. The farmer and his sons jumped off the wagon and began to put out the fire with a well-drilled bucket brigade. The steam rose and the straw sizzled its dying embers as the man and the wife rushed to find with great relief that their children were safe.

As soon as the fire was completely contained, the farmer and his boys rounded up some more tar paper and lumber and quickly repaired enough of the fire damage to make the remaining part of the shack somewhat habitable once more. Even the wind abated, but the approaching darkness and the silence of evening left many questions unresolved.

Supper for the family that evening was more hurried and perfunctory than normal. There seemed to be a need for the children to rest after the harrowing ordeal of the afternoon, and the adults also needed an opportunity to put their heads together and plan for the future.

Lately, all of the important plans had been talked over in bed. Somehow the close intimacy and the body warmth that each offered the other brought a mutual understanding to the couple. Even the children who were old enough to understand what their parents were talking about felt that they were included in this love, and in that way even they were better prepared for the changes that were to follow.

All of these conversations were in Spanish and loud enough for the children to hear. The adults hardly ever referred to each other by name. For emphasis, he might say, "Look here, Mi Viejita," and she might reply, "Yes, Mi Viejo."

"Look here, My Little Old Lady, maybe you should have remained with your parents back in Mexico. Surely the children would have been better off. At least they wouldn't have to be left alone all day."

"No, My Old Man. Why did we get married anyway? Was it so that we could have a life together, or so that we could live apart as we've been doing for most of these last five years. I shall never willingly leave you again. Evidently you don't realize what a penance it is for us women to wait while our men are far away from us. No, sir, from now on it's going to be, 'Until death do us part.'"

"Well, if we must be parted by death, I can only hope and pray that I should go first. I understand better than you know how difficult it must have been for you to live dependent upon your parents during my absence, but the truth of the matter is that I just didn't think I could provide for you and the children at all in Mexico when all I could do was to help herd cattle once in a while.

"Until we were married, I was pretty dependent upon my dad, and although I know how much he loves me, it hurts me to realize that he has always regarded me as quite immature and incapable. That's part of the reason we left him in Montana. I really want to prove to him and to myself that I can handle all of the responsibilities I've undertaken as a man.

"In that respect I'm thankful to you for fulfilling all of your duties as a wife and a mother, and it is for that reason I hope that if ever one of us should have to die, I would prefer that it would be me, because in every sense of the word, you have proven your value to all of us."

"If you really mean that, then I think you should listen closely to what I'm about to suggest. First of all, we should leave this migrant life forever! You're not a farmer like my dad, and I'm very glad that you are not. As I see it, any farmer whether here or in Mexico is rooted to the land. He lavishes more attention to his crops and his animals than he does to his wife and his children.

"Frequently his barns and his fences are kept in better repair than his house. His only vacations come with illness or with death, and even then someone immediately must be ready to take his place because the cows must be milked, the pigs have to be fed, and the crops need to be cultivated.

"I would love for us to be settled down in a city or town. Certainly you could find work that you could do while I stayed home to care for the children. It would make me much happier, and it would free your mind from worry about us. Furthermore, we're very likely to have more children."

"I think you're right, Mi Viejita. Tomorrow morning, I'll go see Roberto Cervantes and his family. They're all through with their topping, and I'm sure that if we offer to pay them, they'll be glad to come help us fulfill our contract."

"Is he the one they call Caruso?"

"Yes, he's really a nice young man. He claims that we're related. He's been trying to talk me into going to Moline, Illinois with him. He says that he has an uncle living there who writes to him regularly. Evidently there are a lot of jobs there waiting for any man that's willing to work."

Early in December, the whole family found itself loaded down with everything they could carry at the Rock Island Railroad station in Estherville, Iowa. Here the man bought their tickets and checked their trunk and a couple of larger bundles to Moline, Illinois. Then they waited in the depot for the train that was to take them to a new way of living.

The yellowish lights had been turned on in the depot, and night had enveloped the building before they heard the plaintive train whistle tweet— tweet— tweet tweet, way off in the distance.

Now each person grabbed his assigned bundle and stepped out into the darkness, being very careful to maintain the correct distance from the railroad tracks.

The tracks glimmered faintly as the headlight from the approaching engine whirled around and around and the incessant ringing of its big brass bell warned them to stay clear of the approaching monster that clanged, wheezing, puffing, and screeching to a stop. Then it shot out a huge cloud of steam as the metal door of one of the coaches banged open. The conductor threw down his small metal stool for them to climb into the coach and find their assigned seats inside the train.

Now the man arranged two seats facing each other, and the woman took two blankets out of one of the large bags she had carried on board. She placed the three older boys in reclining positions on the seats and covered them with the blankets while her husband held the baby. Then she took the baby, told the boys to go to sleep and went to sit in another seat next to her man.

They all closed their eyes, but whatever sleep came upon any of them was fitful at best. The constant rocking motion, the noise, the acceleration and deceleration, as well as the numerous stops to discharge and board different passengers was in no way conducive to peaceful slumber.

The sunlight had begun to paint the eastern sky with streaks of orange and yellow when the oldest boy gave up on any further attempts to sleep. He had tried to relieve his aching bones by turning first on one side and then on the other, but whether he did this or slid up or down on his seat, the result was the same. He just had to stand up and walk around. He got up and began to walk up and down the aisles.

He made a game of going from one end of the coach to another without touching the seats on either side. All of the trainmen seemed to do this without any trouble regardless of how much the train would pitch and roll. He also liked to walk between the coaches, though it scared him to push the bar which opened the air-controlled door with a mighty sucking whoosh.

Most of all he liked to stand in the vestibule between coaches, even though he dreaded the recurring thought that he might suddenly fall and be crushed beneath the wheels. Here he could see the landscape hurtling by. It seemed that he was standing still while the trees, the telephone posts, and even an occasional building went flying past the window as if in a hurry to escape the noise, the smoke, and the general commotion of this huge black snake which went gliding in and around the hills and valleys seeking an indefinite goal.

All night the train had spoken to him in different tongues. When it would start up it would say, "I sure shall go, I sure shall go, I sure shall go, go, go, go, sure go, go, go."

As that message got lost in its faster and faster delivery, some loose brake shoe would proclaim, "Click clack, clickety-clack. Outside its black, but we won't go back, not back, not back, click clack, clickety-clack."

Whenever it came to a stop it would shriek, "Screech, squeak squeal. Ouch my heal! Don't stop in this field. Don't you know how I feel? No more field!"

On one of his many trips to the toilet, to the drinking fountain, to the vestibule, he saw a little shelf that held some brochures. He took one without thinking, and as he perused it he noticed that it was a schedule for that train. From then on he studied the sheet and kept looking outside hoping to find some kind of landmark that would tell him how much farther they would have to go before reaching their destination.

Suddenly there was a loud rattling noise the like of which he had never heard before. It startled him until he noticed the supporting metal cables and the crossed iron beams and bars of the biggest bridge he had ever seen in his whole life. He looked downward into the broadest and muddiest river he had ever seen. The train was actually crossing the river at a great height. It appeared that there were two levels to this bridge. Unbelievingly, it appeared that a street car and some automobiles were traveling along the bridge at the lower level while the train was crossing at the same time immediately above.

Now, surely he must keep his eyes open and see whether he could read the name of the town at the next station. Within minutes the train screeched to another stop, and he noticed a sign on a large yellow brick building that said ROCK ISLAND. The schedule in his hand read ROCK ISLAND, ILLINOIS. The very next stop just had to be the place where they intended to make their new home. Here he would be freed from the daily loneliness and responsibility of watching his brothers from daylight until dusk. Here maybe they could live in a real house and he could go to school. Here maybe they could start the new life that would make his mother happy.

He was so engrossed with these thoughts that he hardly felt the train start up again, and almost immediately afterward it began to slow down in preparation for another stop. The sun was already about a quarter of its way up into the sky when his searching eyes finally fixed on the sign for which he had been searching all morning. There on the highest side of the depot carefully printed in a half circle was the word MOLINE.

As he looked around for his parents who were busily gathering their luggage, he glanced out of the window once more. How clean and bright and beautiful everything seemed. Even though this was December, he imagined that once outside everything would be invitingly warm and pleasant. He was tired of being cooped up in the crowded, noisy train. He longed to step out onto the firm, unmoving ground.

Without realizing that he was talking to himself loudly enough for people around him to hear, he found himself repeating in Spanish one of his family's favorite phrases of thanksgiving, "Alabado sea Dios." Then he added almost as an afterthought, "We're finally here in my Moline."

CHAPTER 2

MAGNETISM

The mighty Mississippi crawls lazily westward, tracing the entire northern boundary of Moline, Illinois. Rock Island forms the western boundary, and East Moline the eastern boundary thus leaving the hills and plains to the south as the only way for the city to extend its growth. This limitation is only geographical! There are no limitations to the growth of Moline in the minds of Moliners.

Moliners will tell strangers that you can get anything in Moline! If not right in Moline, you'll find it in Rock Island, Davenport, somewhere in the Quad Cities, in Chicago, or in some other place in the world to which Moline is tangential.

China means the center of the world (according to the scholarly Dr. Hung Ti Chu); but for real Moliners, their city is the center of the universe. This was true when I first came to Moline in 1925, and I find it still true as I return again and again to revisit the scenes of my boyhood.

We first arrived in December of 1925. My dad was a slim, wiry built, medium-height, dark-complexioned man of 36. My mother was then beginning to gain enough weight so that it was questionable as to whether she was expecting again. Her olive complexion was clear, and her brown eyes had the soft resignation of those who accept their lot as a temporary condition but expect somehow to improve that condition as soon as possible.

She was then 25, and had already borne five children. The second had died in infancy. I was 10, Tom was 6, Leonard was 3, and Mike was still being carried when we walked over the red-bricked passageway toward the Moline depot. The depot was also of red brick, and it fairly glistened a welcome. Then we caught our first glimpse of the LeClaire Hotel. It stood magnificently taller then any building I had ever seen!

The LeClaire Hotel continues to be the tallest building in Moline today, but at that time it also represented the highest in social and cultural achievement. The well-to-do of the entire area held their most important meetings in the Top Hat. This was the ballroom on the highest floor from which the mighty could look down upon the lowliest Moliners as they gaped in bewildered awe at the bellboys in maroon and white uniforms, rushing baggage in and out of the LeClaire Hotel.

The LeClaire Theatre stood next door. Its plush interior, its magnificent stage, balcony, and other appointments bespoke of a grandeur unparalleled in the entertainment world. On the outside wall a new sign had been painted proclaiming the advent of SINGING TALKING PICTURES. However, the stage shows were still its main attraction. Daisy and Violet Hilton, the Siamese twins, came here to put on a demonstration of dancing and romancing, and spectators flocked to enjoy another proof that, "Moline has everything!"

As in all stage shows of that era, there was a variety of entertainment. The Hilton sisters probably did the least and were appreciated the most. They were young, charming, and enigmatic. A narrator introduced each of their acts with voluble description of their anatomical liaison. He included considerable highly personal detail that was probably embarrassing to the girls. The curious were particularly interested in the fact that one of the twins was fond of alcohol while the other was not. However, the effects of its consumption by one made the other just as drunk as the imbiber.

It was also pointed out that one of the girls was somewhat promiscuous. Again, not only was her twin equally aroused by whatever feelings were started by the first, but of course she would have to be present at whatever lovemaking might have ensued. Years later, the local newspapers ran stories of their marital adventures. Most of the problems of being joined physically and emotionally had been obstacles too great for these girls. Unlike Chang and Eng, their unhappiness far outweighed their happiness. Many Moliners remembered the Hilton sisters, although I doubt that these twins remembered Moline.

The movies continued to challenge the stage shows. Their titles were titillating. *The Golden Bed*, *Tiger Love*, *Wolves of the Night*, and *Unguarded Women* are examples of a week's offering. The LeClaire Theatre ran a big advertisement in the *Moline Daily Dispatch* which promised, "For one week, starting Sunday, a fearless handling of vital problems today." Then in opposite columns, "Her strongest weakness was love, the story of a typical American Girl," and, "Captain of his soul, or a slave of his desires? A story of new morals and old."

The competition for the movie entertainment patronage was intense. Beside the LeClaire, there were also the following theaters in Moline: the Mirror, Bio, American, Lyric, Avoy (on the hill), Burtis, Palance, Plaza, and Orpheum. So in addition to stage shows, the LeClaire Hotel also advertised the LeClaire Orchestra with Ceno Peterson, director, and William E. Beasley at the Le-Claire organ. Occasionally, they also had Charleston dance contests at which loving cups and other prizes were offered to the amateur contestants.

Across the street, on the corner of 18th Street stood another brick building several stories high. While not so imposing, it always had a steady stream of youth entering and leaving its eastern entrance and an occasional trickle of older persons doing likewise at its northern doorway. The most important attribute of this beehive of activity as far as I was concerned was a glass-covered bulletin sign whose mast-head heralded the fact that "The Moline YMCA is proud of its young men and boys." I never passed that sign without swelling my chest a little higher with pride, realizing implicitly that the sign included me in a very special way. MOLINE was the important word, and I was a Moliner justly deserving of that pride.

Immediately west was the *Moline Daily Dispatch* building, where baseball scores were prominently displayed in the windows inning by inning. The last building on that side of the street was the Moline Public Library. Its wide steps, Grecian columns, and the sign over its entrance bespoke of Moline's recognition by Andrew Carnegie.

Downtown Moline meant any of the four corners of 5th Avenue and 15th Street. I always had the feeling of entering downtown as I walked westward on 5th Avenue past the LeClaire Hotel on 19th Street, and I always felt that I had gone through downtown after I had passed the First Lutheran Church and Esterdahl's Mortuary on 13th Street.

I ambled contentedly along this path hundreds of times. At least once per week I walked from 25th Street to 10th Street where St. Mary's Catholic Church is located on 4th Avenue. Actually,

T J E D

T L F

T J C

3x Sea Trout

2x Lamb

3x Jelly

2x Chee

The National Trust
Castle-a-Rede
1194 Whitepark Rd
Ballintoy
Antrim
BT54 6LS

Booking Ref: 77777

Cash Customer

VAT No   GB 239 5031 67
Date   26/07/2018
Time   11:48
Till   01/10005l399
Session   1300010450

Currency   GBP

ITEM	QTY	VAT	GROSS

12.30-13.30 (26/07/18) @ 12:15

Adult Standard   1   1.33   8.00

TOTAL (Inc Vat)   8.00
NET   6.67
VAT   1.33

CASH TOTAL   8.00
TOTAL TENDERED   10.00
CHANGE DUE(Base Currency)   2.00

Your sale was processed by Ricky
Join today & enjoy free entry to over
500 properties
Free Wi-Fi available
Thank you for supporting our work

* 10005l399 *

3rd Avenue or the railroad tracks would have been a more direct route, but I always chose to go through downtown to enjoy whatever excitement might be downtown that day.

Sometimes the rewards were great! One day, a man who called himself "The Human Fly" scaled the outer wall of the LeClaire Hotel by pulling himself vertically from window to window. Our hearts popped into our mouths when momentarily he seemed to lose his grip or footing, but when he finally pulled himself onto the top of the roof, we cheered with appreciative relief.

Radio was just beginning as another great entertainer. One day, while walking past Rank's shoe store, I became an unwitting participant of a "man-on-the-street" program. The question of the day was, "Approximately how many pounds of food does the average individual consume during a 30-year period of time?"

The rest of the participants were anxious to know whether the consumer was young or old, large or small, poverty-stricken or wealthy, vegetarian or meat eater, etc. Most of them wisely hedged on their answers or gave highly qualified replies. Suddenly, I was called to the microphone, asked to identify myself, and given an opportunity to answer the question of the day. Without thought or hesitation I replied, "Three hundred pounds."

I was quite proud of myself as I walked away. I even wondered that I might be invited again to display my wisdom. Subsequently, I was amazed at how many of my acquaintances had heard me on the radio, and how ignorant they considered that my reply had been. Needless to say, I did not appear again on the radio for a long, long time.

The people of Moline were most ingratiating. We arrived in Moline after choosing this destination on the purest whim. When we worked in the sugarbeet fields of Montana and Iowa, we had seen again and again that enigmatic emblem of a deer jumping over a fallen stump and the words warmly proclaiming:

John Deere
Moline, Ill.

We had noted this decal on all the green-painted farm tractors and implements. The same emblem was to be found on the walls of farm implement repair shops, implement dealer stores, and garages. Dad's conclusion must have been that all of this notoriety must include a great population that richly deserved this widespread fame. It did.

Just how he managed to meet Lazaro Sanchez I never did know. I remember leaving Mother and my three brothers at the depot, walking past the LeClaire Hotel, holding tightly to my father's fingers, and returning to the station with a quart of milk, a bag of bananas, and a package of Fig Newtons. We also returned for our worldly possessions which we had left in a few bulging handbags, because now we knew that we'd spend that evening in the attic of Lazaro Sanchez's house at 2433 4th Avenue. Actually, we spent the next three nights there.

My dad got a job immediately in a stone quarry on 34th Street and 5th Avenue. The question arose as to where we would be staying next. Our experiences in the beet fields had always included some kind of housing provided by the beet farmer, but now, we knew that we must find a rental someplace.

The house next-door to Sanchez stood empty. There was no FOR RENT sign, and both Dad and Lazaro agreed that this type of house would probably not be available for Mexicans. Mother and I put our hopes ahead of our anticipated rejection, and when Dad went to work, we stepped out into the first heavy snowfall of the year in search of the owner of the house. The search appeared hopelessly futile. Neither Mother nor I had ever been involved in such activities, but mysteriously, at the end of the day we started moving in. This house at 2437 4th Avenue continued to be our mailing address for many years, although we lived there only a few brief, happy months.

We stayed in that warm, lovely house for as long as Dad worked in the stone quarry. It was ample for our needs. A large cool basement was accessible through a set of stairs that came up through a trap door into a closet in the center of the house. There was also a set of sloping hinged doors covering steps for an outside access.

The foundation of the house included several small windows for ventilation and one for the coal chute. In those days, Moline Consumers delivered ice in the summer and coal in the winter by horse-drawn wagons. The ice was brought into the kitchen by a man who carried a large block on his back with a pair of huge ice tongs. The coal was shoveled onto a slick metal slide that extended from the back of the wagon into the window-like opening to the basement where the coal was stored near the furnace.

The second floor of the house contained two large bedrooms, heated quite adequately by the chimney that came up through the center of the house and between these two bedrooms. The main floor had a large kitchen, an adjoining full bathroom with the first bathtub I had ever seen, outside of the ones I had seen in hotels. There were also two small bedrooms and a fair sized living room with the front door in the center opening up to 4th Avenue. The house was so large, in fact, that we later rented the upstairs bedrooms to another family named Cervantes whose American mother had evidently left the father with two sub-teenaged children named Alfred and Opal.

Unfortunately, this proud and ample existence didn't last long. I had just begun to get used to the wonders of the barn in back of the house in a yard that extended a full block to the railroad tracks when I heard that Dad had found work as a section hand for the DRI&NW (Davenport, Rock Island, and Northwestern Railroad).

That line somehow used trackage of the CM&StP. (Chicago, Milwaukee, and St. Paul Railroad). However, its main business seemed to provide spur tracks into the many factories that were springing up near the river. This line also did much of the switching necessary to bring in raw materials and ship out finished goods on the three main lines, which in order of their importance were the CRI&P, the CB&Q and the CM&StP. Dad simply called them the Rock Island, the Burlington, and the Milwaukee roads.

I vaguely understood why Dad wanted to get out of the stone quarry. He had spent all of his life in the great outdoors. First, briefly as a cowboy in Mexico, then following his father in needless adventures; traveling from La Piedad, Michoacán, Mexico, northward across the United States, into Canada. They worked briefly as section hands, but they worked only to earn enough money to move on to the next place.

I guess the quarry was too dark, too damp, and mostly too confining. One thing was immediately made clear: the wages on the railroad would not permit us to continue paying rent. In those days, the railroads nearly always provided some kind of minimum housing for their section workers. So we prepared to leave our lovely house in order to move into a boxcar east of 25th Street, right between the Milwaukee and the Burlington tracks. However, just before we left, we sublet the upstairs rooms to the Ortiz family; Goya, Tony, Caroline, Rosa, and "Childo." The understanding was that they were to continue renting that house, and that we would continue to get our mail at 2437 4th Avenue. This arrangement continued for the next 10 years.

My brief sojourn in a real house left me ashamed of having to live cooped up in a two-room boxcar. I fantasized all kinds of dreams about digging a lovely home beneath that squalid exterior, and having the boxcar be but an entry to a magnificent subterranean home where only my closest friends would know and have access to our real living quarters.

I also fantasized owning a very small convertible automobile. I would carefully choose one of my friends, and we would dash from my hidden subterranean driveway out onto 5th Avenue. Then we would drive downtown to Lagomarcino's where we would both order big cherry sodas. Of course, I would be treating.

Then we would drive slowly back home, basking in the euphoria of knowing that many of my schoolmates would have seen me on the way to town and back. Now, surely they would be marveling at the style and dignity of my life, and maybe they would also wonder at how I might have reached such attainments. Occasionally, I even thought I might throw some big, elaborate parties for all of my schoolmates. In those days, in my dreams, everything seemed possible. Moline was my land of limitless opportunity.

The population of Moline as of December 31, 1925 was 34,756. Times were good. The stock market set higher records almost daily. Business was good among Moline merchants. Many new homes were under construction, and it seemed that anyone could have a job just for the asking.

My Dad had invited my Uncle Juan Trujillo to come to Moline from Cuyler, Texas where they had previously worked together on a railroad section gang. Dad and Juan had been boyhood friends, and Juan's marriage to Dad's sister Cristina further cemented that friendship. The Trujillos not only came quickly to Moline, but they also moved into another boxcar just a few feet east of the one we lived in.

I remember that it had been empty when we moved in, and that we had used it as a one-night breeding stall for a nanny goat which we kept tethered along various grassy spots near the railroad tracks. We kept her for a while, but the bother of finding new feeding places and bringing her water was not really worth the trouble. Anyway, I never really cared for goat's milk or for its meat.

Our life in the boxcar needs some further explanation. There were four boxcars just east of 25th Street. Two of them were between the main tracks of the Milwaukee and the Burlington Companies. We made our home in one, and my uncle and aunt lived in the other one.

A few feet north of the last Milwaukee tracks were two more boxcars. The Florencio Ramirez family lived in one, and my second cousin, Dolores Cervantes, eventually came to live in the other one when Dad got him a job with the railroad. Just west of that boxcar was the section tool shed where the section hands met to begin and end their days' work.

A two-hole outhouse was located just east of the tool shed. This comprised the toilet facilities for all of us residents of the boxcars, the other section hands, and for their foreman, George Kakavas.

Water for washing and cooking was another matter. There was a water line about a half block west of our boxcar just on the other side of 25th Street. An outlet valve there provided drinking water for all the crews of the switching engines, for the section workmen of all four railroad lines, for the residents of our boxcars as well as for the residents of the boxcars west of 25th Street, and even for old Mr. Melin.

Dolores and Octaviano Cervantes

He was the crossing guard who had a small guard's shack in the center of all the railroad lines. In those days, most major railroad crossings for automobiles had a guard who stayed in his little shack all day. As the trains approached the street crossing, he came out with a stop sign in hand to warn the motorists of the oncoming train traffic. It was quieter than the automatic bells of later years, and as a safety factor it was probably more effective.

In any event, carrying water became my chief household chore. I accomplished this by lugging two 12-quart pails full of water from that source to our boxcar as often as necessary, which was at least twice daily. When I got the water home, the first pail went on top of the only table we had, and a long-handled dipper was put into it for drinking. The other pail went under the table.

That water was used sparingly for washing the dishes and for our daily ablutions. We used the same small wash basin for both of these purposes. Then we threw the water out of the front door, and this helped to keep down the dust of the passing trains.

Saturdays were generally devoted to washing clothes in the morning and to taking baths in the afternoon. This meant that I had to carry water most of that day. For these twin purposes we had two round, galvanized metal tubs. First, I had to make a wood fire outside within a circle of rocks. Next, I put the well-blackened tub over the fire, emptied into it whatever water we might have on hand in the two pails, then I proceeded to rush back and forth between the water valve and our boxcar until both tubs and both pails were full.

Mother would then boil her clothes in one tub. When the water cooled down she'd scrub them on a washboard. Then finally she'd rinse them in the other tub and hang them on a clothes line nearby. This whole laundry operation was usually an out-of-doors job, and needless to say, all of the used water was dumped nearby.

As soon as the water was dumped, I started carrying water again, and I filled all four receptacles to overflowing once more. This time, the rinse tub was brought into the house, and the bathing-the-family ritual began. The water was always cool. Only in the really cold weather did we warm the water on the same wood burning stove that we also used for cooking and heating.

The younger children were bathed first. The smallest ones were sponged off in the wash basin, and all of the rest of us, including Mother and Dad, took turns soaping up in the tub and rinsing off with the dipper which went in and out of the pails of clean water.

When Dad and Mother finally finished their baths, and after I had filled the pails for the last time, then we were ready for the walk to St. Mary's Church and confession. After confession we came back home to eat an especially hearty supper. The requirements for receiving Holy Communion on the following day, besides being in the state of grace, was complete abstinence from food and drink from midnight until receiving the Holy Sacrament on the following morning. I think that remaining in the state of grace was more difficult for me than the fasting, but we always attended the earlier Masses.

The reality away from the tracks continued to be rewarding. I had enrolled in the 4th grade at Grant School on 25th Street and 7th Avenue. It was a reasonably close walk, but I fairly flew over the railroad tracks in hopes no one would see where I really lived, until I was safely among the houses I considered proper.

Once away from the tracks, I moved within another world. That uneasiness of living in a boxcar was as quickly forgotten as I had left behind me the long, lonely days in the beet fields of Montana and northern Iowa. City life agreed with me in every way! The Fackaldys, who owned the grocery store next to Mengel's Market on 25th Street and 5th Avenue, as well as the Feeleys, who owned another grocery store across from the Fackaldys, had quickly extended us credit. Later, Frank DeJaeger also gave us credit at his hardware store on 23rd Street and 5th Avenue. Now our name was written on a pad of bills at each of those stores. All we had to do was ask for what we needed and charge it.

Our Moline grocers, Peter and Jennie Taets, circa 1943. Their son Paul is on the tricycle.

When Peter F. Taets and his wife Jennie took over the Feeley's store, they also took over our credit. In retrospect, I'm amazed at the trust with which we were treated by Moline merchants and other townspeople. I remember buying on my own credit a wagon, a pair of shoe skates for ice skating, and a new bicycle. I was 12 years of age when I made these time-payment purchases. They were made without security or interest, other than my word. It should also be noted that the bicycle was an Excelsior that cost

$38.00, or approximately two weeks' normal earnings for my father on his railroad job.

Our good credit rating had only one unfortunate result. Dad had taken a co-worker to a small clothing store on 17th Street and 5th Avenue, where credit was quickly given to him on Dad's recommendation. This man soon left his job and his debts. When Dad found out about this, he and I promptly presented ourselves before the merchant and told him what had happened.

My dad insisted on making good the entire amount owed by his former co-worker. The merchant seemed unwilling for Dad to pay this debt, but he finally accepted. On the way out of the store, my dad said to the merchant, "Not only will I never again recommend another man's credit, but I won't buy anything on credit myself." At this, the merchant implored Dad to take back his money, but Dad was adamant. As far as I know, he stuck to his word.

I loved to go to the store for my mother. I soon discovered that although we had moved into a city whose population was mostly Protestant, the Fackaldys, the DeJaegers, and the Feeleys were not only Catholic, but they were also recognized to be among the "pillars" of St. Mary's Church.

Steve Feeley treated me like a younger brother. Frank DeJaeger used to bless me with the sign of the cross and proclaim his hopes loudly that I might become a priest. Even the neighbors along the way seemed unusually kind. I simply adored a young woman who always greeted me with a cheery "Hi-yaah!" I always considered that to be a special greeting invented just for me. I even struggled to come up with a similarly inventive response, but I never managed any more than a weak but appreciative, "Hullo!"

There was only one place along the way where I was made to feel unwelcome. Two boys of approximately my age lived in a dilapidated, small house at the end of 24th Street and 4th Avenue. I always slowed down here on my way home to catch a last full whiff of the delectable aroma emanating from the National Licorice Factory in the next block. Several times as I lingered slowly past their house, one of the boys would come out to announce, "We can't have company today." I never knew what to reply.

My parents had always sent me on small errands since I was five years old. After I was 10, I did much of the grocery shopping for milk, meat, and other sundries, but it only occurred to me once that I could stop and play along the way. It never happened again. I was victimized by an older boy, but the lesson that was taught me was worth several times the money which I lost that day.

Mother had sent me to the meat market with a dollar and some change so that we could have some meat for supper. This was a rare treat in our house, and a dollar was a lot of money for us. Usually I charged our purchases, but this particular market had a cash and carry policy. Just outside of the market I met a fast-talking young man who soon found out not only what my errand was but also how much money I had. He invited me to come play with him in his yard. I knew that Dad would not return from work for a good three or four hours. Still, I should have been warier when he said, "We'll have to take the street car, because I live in East Moline."

"That's too far," I objected.

"I have swings, a teeter-totter, and all kinds of things. Besides, it won't take long, and you'll never miss the nickel for the street car ride."

The latter was true. I knew Mother and Dad were reasonably generous, so in a show of bravado, I replied, "O.K. Let's take the street car. I'll even pay the nickel for your fare, too."

We arrived at his home on the hilltop where East Moline's first high school was built later. He swung me on the swings. We teeter-tottered, wrestled, laughed, and had a great time.

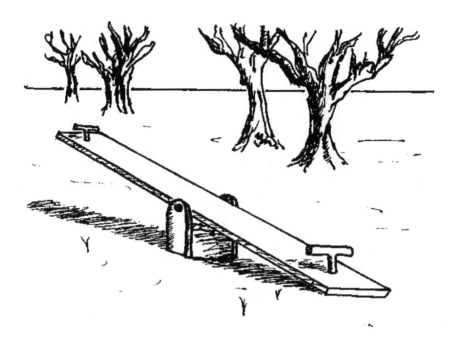

Suddenly, I discovered that my dollar was gone! It struck me then that my host might have taken it as he pushed me on the swing or as we wrestled on the grassy knoll. At once I became aware of the fact that my dad received his pay check twice a month. Often he would cash it and send me to the store to pay our bill. Hardly ever did this bill exceed fifteen dollars for the two-week period. I was missing the grocery money for at least one day's subsistence.

"I've lost the dollar", I announced gingerly. "Have you seen it?"

"No," he answered nonchalantly, "But I'll help you look for it."

Then the search began. For me it was a frenzy of wild activity! My host seemed to look casually and without any real concern. As I noticed his apparent nonchalance, resentment boiled up within me. I recalled that he had been in the house. No one was at home. Finally, in desperation, I demanded that he let me search him.

"O.K.," he said as he turned his pockets inside out. "I didn't take your dollar. It must have dropped out of your pocket and got blown away by the wind."

I realized that the logic was sound, but the wind was weak, and my belief in him even weaker.

Finally, we gave up the search. Without a word, I walked down the hill and caught the streetcar for home. To the soft click-clacking of the wheels, I concocted a story to the effect that I had given the butcher the dollar bill as he weighed the meat. I blamed him for putting the bill into the cash register and for forgetting that I had paid him in advance. I even insisted to my parents that I was to return the following day when the market had checked its receipts. For good measure, I returned two days, and I'll never know whether my parents believed my story, any more than I believed my playmate's.

I'm sure that my salvation that day was due to Mother's ability to come up with a wonderful meatless meal. She served us re-fried beans, fried potatoes, scrambled together with eggs, fresh green beans, and a tantalizing sauce of garden-ripe tomatoes, cooked chilies, and chopped green onions, all of which was made most palatable when she uncovered a basket of hot freshly made flour tortillas. Everyone's attack on the meal effectively stopped all the questions, and the euphoria of contentment following the feast turned away all needless doubts.

The corner of 23rd Street and 5th Avenue held a particularly magnetic appeal for me. Here A.W. Kortkamp established a large tent for Pentecostal revival meetings. "It's the old-time religion, it's the old time religion, it's the old time religion, and it's good enough for me." Few could resist the soulful, toe-tapping melodies calling upon the sinners to repent and accept God. The period of individual prayer and public confession was irresistible.

Sometimes I wondered whether the sinner did not exaggerate in order to win a better acceptance from his fellow worshippers. How different this was from the dark, foreboding confessional at St. Mary's Church! There you had to search your conscience in the quiet, lugubrious semi-darkness of the church. The other confessors there did not know that you were silently planning to tell all to God (who knew), while minimizing the extent and seriousness of the sins to the priest (who didn't know, but who would ask the searching questions and assess the penance).

At St. Mary's, sins were furtive and shameful, while at the tent they seemed to be proof of repentance and love. It would be an exercise in academic futility to determine where the penitent was sincerer. There's no doubt as to where repentance was more dramatic. Many who came to scoff at the tent services, remained to pray. Each evening there would be a parade of faithful coming forward to receive Jesus and to be healed.

Sometimes, Mother used to make me take Tom with me on various errands. This I disliked not only because it limited my freedom, but because I never really knew how our childhood adventures would turn out. Almost invariably, after we stopped at the tent, Tom would stagger into our little kitchen mimicking the latest convert.

"I am a drunken sinner," he would blubber in an attempt to portray a tipsy man.

"I beat my wife, and ran off with another woman. I now repent that I didn't do this much sooner!"

Dad always laughed at Tom's mischief-making. Mother would try to correct him, and I cringed with fear that he might blurt out other sins which might really tend to betray him, or embarrass both of us.

One day when I had gone to DeJaeger's, Frank said to me, "Jack, your brother Tom stole an alarm clock. After you left I looked for it, and it was gone."

"Are you sure?" I asked incredulously.

"I'm almost positive," Frank replied. "While I was writing up your bill, I saw Tom picking up an alarm clock. After you left, I looked for it, and it was gone."

"Well, I don't know," I sputtered. "I just don't know that Tom would do that."

"Well, don't tell your dad. Just tell Tom that he must return it, and we'll forget all about it."

I left the store in dazed disbelief. Dad and Mother's sense of righteous honesty had never been preached or questioned. It was always assumed by me that only criminals stole, and I couldn't see my own brother as a criminal. Nevertheless, I walked home hurriedly and immediately confronted Tom.

"Frank DeJaeger said you stole a clock from his store," I accused. "Did you?"

"No," Tom answered feebly, "I just took it."

"Well," I fired back indignantly, "Where is it?"

"In the trunk. Right here," he said as he brought the clock out still safely ensconced in its display case.

"Now, you'll just have to take it back," I muttered threateningly, and with this order, Tom's face dissolved into a penitential torrent of sobs and tears.

Immediately, I was overwhelmed with sympathy for him. While I could not begin to guess why he had taken it, I could thoroughly understand his reticence at returning the clock. We stood and looked at each other in quiet discomfort. Finally I offered, "Come on, I'll go with you."

Suddenly, he brightened up, dried his tears with the back of his hand, and we walked slowly to DeJaeger's. Here, Tom and I waited until all the customers were gone. Then, without a word, Tom offered up the clock to Frank with outstretched hands. I remember vaguely trying to make some kind of apology. Maybe none was needed.

Tom continued to be an enigma for me the rest of his life. His clowning caricatures enlivened the friendly relations he had among many Moliners, but his peccadillos caused him many Pagliacci-like confessions. Even in his religious observances he was irrepressible, and Dad half-angrily, half-lovingly predicted that Tom would probably become a Protestant someday.

Going with the family to movies, the circus, or the carnival were occasional treats. Most of the time, Dad and I would scout these events in advance, and if we determined that the younger kids would behave, we'd then take Mother and the rest of the family.

We always enjoyed the stage shows best, and we were quite sorry to see them lose out to the "talkies." *Journey's End* became our first acceptable substitute for staged drama. The Little Rascals and Laurel & Hardy comedies subsequently provided the light entertainment of the vaudeville comedians, but nothing in Moline ever again replaced those thrilling moments when the grand drapes parted and the speaker's curtain went up in the LeClaire Theatre. Footlights up, lavish stage settings, and those moving colorful spotlights could transform the dreariest day into a temporary heaven-on-earth as the music swelled out from the cavernous orchestra pit.

As we grew up, our taste for movies had us making personal heroes of certain actors. Halfway up the western side of 15th

Street, just north of the 5th Avenue alley was a small theater that specialized in cowboy movies. Its name, The American, had a particular appeal for me. So, we watched the cowboy pictures whose plots frequently included Mexican antagonists. I never saw anything particularly wrong in that. Maybe my brothers didn't either.

My favorite cowboy was Jack Hoxie, Tom's was Tom Mix, and Leonard liked Al Wilson. The only disagreement among us three brothers was the moot question as to which of our heroes would win if they should ever become involved in a fight. Needless to say, we never saw them in the same movie.

There was another movie theater on the southeast corner of 15th Street and 6th Avenue. It was called The Mirror, but we seldom went there. We had other less expensive recreations, particularly during the summertime.

The northernmost end of 25th Street stopped at the river's bank. Here, the Moline Consumers Company stored its building sand. We watched its dredging by giant cranes from the middle of the stream. Then it was loaded onto flat barges and finally dumped into mountainous piles of coarse, wet, reddish-brown granules.

My brothers and I would race each other barefooted to the top of each succeeding peak. The higher we went, the greater the struggle to lift each leg out from the finer, drier, less-packed sand. Once at the summit, we played king-of-the-hill and eventually ended up rolling over and over to the bottom of the pile.

Occasionally, we would jump onto the barges moored next to the sand pile. Sometimes Dad and Mother would come with us, and we watched while the two of them went swimming in the river. We gaped in awe at the bunny-like leaps Mother used to propel herself through the water. Dad was a good swimmer, and he moved out toward the center of the stream with strong, powerful strokes. As he came shoreward, he appeared to be rowing himself first with one arm and quickly with the other, his head and half of his chest protruding like a Viking ship homeward bound! Nevertheless, I was always apprehensive about his safety until he walked out of the water.

Late one hot, sticky afternoon, Mother gave Tom and me permission to go play in the sand. Somehow, it wasn't much fun for just the two of us. Our exertions of running and tumbling made the heat even more oppressive. The sand stuck to our legs, and we decided to wash it off in the river. Eventually, we took off our trousers and began to frolic around in the water. Tom couldn't swim at all, and I could just barely dog-paddle myself afloat. Without much thought, I began to build mud castles on the shore as Tom continued to splash around in water that gently lapped up about knee-deep. Soon I was aware only of the occasional slap-slap of a lazy wave.

I wasn't really alarmed when I heard the cry, "Jack, help!" Tom was always quite a clown! However, I did turn to reprimand him, and was petrified when I didn't see him. A few feet from where he should have been, my eyes became riveted on a log drifting toward the sand barges. Suddenly, Tom's black head popped up and one hand vainly reached for the log. In a flash I conjectured that he must have mounted the log, got pulled into the deep water by the force of the stream, and he didn't get off until it drifted to where the water was over his head. It was then that he must have yelled.

A second scream broke my momentary paralysis and I became an unthinking blur of activity. In retrospect, I believe that all of my subsequent actions were pure reflex. I ran on the bank downstream, jumped on the first sand barge and got there in time to see the log approaching. Wildly I jumped into the water, thrashing my arms about, and wondrously closed my right fist onto a handful of hair. Holding my breath and clutching the hair in a vise-like grip, I submerged until I touched bottom, then I pushed myself toward the shore. I tried to take a step or two, then I came up for air. I must have done this several times before I could finally hold my head and my right hand out of water and walk to shore. As I reached the edge of the bank, I heard Tom sputter and cough. Then I half fainted from pure exhaustion and relief.

The sun burned down on our half-dressed bodies, and my head throbbed as I focused my eyes on the kaleidoscopic pattern that included Tom slowly rising on one knee and vomiting water. Who knows how long we were there! Almost in a dream we straggled home to a late supper and a grilling on how we had gotten so wet.

There were two parks the whole family visited. Prospect Park we reached by taking the street car at 25th Street and transferring at 15th Street. Then we went south up the hill to the end of the line and walked the last few blocks. The main attraction there was the swimming pool nestled at the bottom of its several hills. Originally, this must have been a small lake created by the run-off rain from the adjoining hills. As I remember it, however, there was a rather large dressing area and concession stand at one end, a small wading pool, and a high diving platform in the middle of the lake. I went swimming there only a few times. I was always afraid that I couldn't make it to the diving tower, and when I did, I always worried that I couldn't make it back.

Riverside Park was our favorite, both summer and winter. It was situated on a gradually sloping area between the cemetery on the south and 4th Avenue on the north. It began for us right next to the fire station on the corner of 27th Street and 4th Avenue and ran diagonally southeasterly to an indefinite boundary just east of the mausoleum. This park was within easy walking distance for us. So, whenever the weather was right, the whole family would go there.

We children would swing on the swings, watch the fishing in the lake, play on the teeter-totters or sit quietly with Mom and Dad under the shade of some big elm tree. All, except Tom. He'd invariably find something exciting to do. Like the day he fell out of a tall tree and landed right beside the rest of us. The fall rendered him unconscious, and for a while we feared he might have been killed, or at least seriously injured. However, he regained consciousness and never seemed to have suffered further from that fall.

That park continued to be the center of our family's summer recreation activities for as long as I lived in Moline. It was here that I started to play football. On crisp fall Saturdays, 40 or 50 of us boys would gather behind the mausoleum and choose up sides. All of us would get to play in a mass mayhem of struggling arms and legs pursuing some tattered old football that bounced crazily as befitted its knobby shape. It was here, too, that I learned to hit a golf ball with a 4-iron which I bought secondhand, and which for 20 years remained as my favorite club. Still, the place that gave me my greatest boyhood thrills was the frozen lake at Riverside Park.

Just before we moved into the boxcar, Mother gave birth to her first baby girl. Dad pretended to his friends that he was disappointed after fathering five boys, but his pride was impossible to hide, and he named her Margaret, after some girl who had been in love with him before he married Mother.

As with all of the rest of his children, excepting Mary, there was no doctor in attendance, neither before, during, nor after the birth. Just which one of our friends sent a visiting nurse to see Mother, none of us really ever knew. I just remember that eventually, we were taking Margaret to be weighed, measured, and examined at the King's Daughters quarters on the second floor of a sandstone building on the northwest corner of 16th street and 3rd Avenue. The first floor of this building contained a secondhand store of clothing and other household objects, and it was here that I bought my first pair of clamp-type ice skates.

The fire station on 27th Street was a favorite spot for many of us. The firemen permitted us to come in, put on our skates, return occasionally to warm ourselves, and to take our skates off. I used to skate at every opportunity when the ice was right, and I fairly wept when I recognized the slushy ice that forecast the end of another winter and the warming days of spring.

Crisply cold, invigorating winter days in Moline were always a special delight for me. Particularly if I could see a cloud of steam at every breath and hear crunching sounds of snow at every step. Occasionally when the ice was too rough for skating at the park, I'd take my skates and go to the river. Here I would find the sand piles covered with snow and once in a while I enjoyed the rare treat of watching the Consumers Company harvest ice from the mighty sleeping Mississippi. It seemed a marvel of simple ingenuity.

Way out toward the center of the river, but considerably upstream from the huge barn-like ice house, men, horses, and equipment were somehow cutting great thick blocks of ice. These were directed into a narrow ice-free channel of water, and floated downstream and shoreward toward a wooden ramp. Here, other men pushed the ice blocks with long spikes onto a series of movable ramps running directly into the ice house.

Now, the blocks of ice were nestled into a bedding of straw, each one being completely straw covered, then others were stacked layer upon layer until the ice house was full. Some ice would last until next winter.

Yet I never skated in that part of the river. Tom's brush with drowning, my apprehension with Dad's swimming, my remembrance of the power of the summer river's current, plus all of the stories I had heard about breaking through an ice bubble and being dragged under the ice, gave me a fear of skating there that no amount of enticing smooth ice surfaces could overcome. Always, I went back to the park lake.

Whenever the ice and weather were just right on a weekend, the park lake was crowded with Moliners from all walks of life. I had always been aware of the haves and the have-nots. Prior to coming to Moline, I had frequently heard my grandfather and my dad talk about "el patron." This always referred to some land owner with kind of feudal rights over his workers. I never noticed any resentment or envy over this arrangement. It was just a fact of life.

It was in Moline that I first noted a sense of social stratification. It first struck me that the more ordinary people lived closer to the river, and that those of a higher order lived on the crests of the surrounding hills. Kenny Gibson, Betty McDannel, and Rosemary Temple climbed the hills on the way home from Grant School with more than half of the students going in that same upward direction. Frank Hample, Alston Roberts, Margaret Castle, and I went in the opposite direction. I ended up closest to the river and between two sets of railroad tracks.

Ice skating, like school, was a common denominator. Here we met, played hockey with bent sticks and tin cans, cracked the whip, and played tag and "I got it" with reckless abandon and complete disregard for the safety of the more sedate skaters. Once in a great while we stopped in our tracks to watch an outstanding skater. Kenny Gibson's mother was one of the best! Dressed in a short skirt of dark velvet with a matching and tight fitting long-

sleeved blouse, she would go through the school figures grace-
fully, swirling that little skirt so that it stood out like a hooped-
dress in a perfect circle around her lithe, slender body.

Few people then had figure skates. Most of us had clamp-type
or hockey-shoe skates, and we'd watch for the serrated points of
the few who did have the figure skates, for we knew that in some
quiet corner of the lake, sooner or later, they'd practice their figure
eights, flying Dutchmen leaps, and spins that the more daring of
us would later seek to emulate. Alston Roberts was especially
adept. After watching Mrs. Gibson, he and I would find an un-
cluttered part of the lake. Then he would seek to go through her
whole routine, and attempt to embellish upon it with a few dancing steps of his own invention.

I liked Alston Roberts. His family moved into the house just
east of 2437 4th Avenue after we had moved into the boxcar. He
was one of my very few school chums that knew where I lived. I
guess they were more or less in the same poverty bracket as my
family was. They had formerly lived in Texas. His older brother
was named Huston.

I even tried to get Alston a job as a caddy, but work was not a
part of his nature. I was riding him on the front frame of my bicycle one day when he purposely stuck his foot into the front wheel
spokes, breaking about three of them and tearing his shoe apart.

I never saw him alive thereafter. When I called on him to go
skating about a week after the incident, his mother calmly told me
that a nail in his torn shoe had started blood poisoning in his foot,
and that he had suddenly died. I was desolated by his loss, partly
because he had been such a close friend, but mostly due to his
sudden and irrevocable demise. It always seemed to me that his
passing was too prosaic and unmarked. He was tall, blonde, and
handsome. He had been trying to talk a slightly older neighboring
girl into a youthful tryst. She rejected him with understanding

logic. Alston was in no way discouraged or seemingly disappointed. He had the rosy optimism of a free spirit. In his every move he was graceful, pleasant, and nonchalant. Shakespeare might well have said of him also that he, "should have died hereafter."

After his death, I skated mostly by myself. I raced around and around that lake trying to outdistance a cold and lonely fury. Later, I participated in the roughest games of ice hockey and crack-the-whip. This relentless drive was finally slowed down one day when I went skating straight from school without going home to ask for permission.

It happened almost immediately upon arrival. A large group of boys in their late teens were terrifying the rest of the skaters. The first skater in line skated from one end of the lake toward the other end, and the rest hooked on one after another by hanging on to the hips of the skater in front with both hands. Whenever the front skater reached his maximum speed, he'd turn to the left or the right sharply, serving as an anchor for the rest of the whip line which would snap in several places sending the last skaters careening all over the lake.

The danger to the rest lay in the uncertainty as to when the whip was to be snapped, as well as in the helpless speed at which those at the end of the whip would be catapulted. It was no wonder then that other boys were trying to break up the whip by breaking through the center of the line before the whip gathered speed.

I was in the center of the line when someone smashed into my right elbow and skated in front of me as I became separated from the line and lurched around trying to regain my balance. Stunned by the force of the blow, I marveled that I had not fallen. Then I almost fainted with horror at looking down at my elbow and failing to see the lower part of my arm and hand. Wildly, I looked around on the ice fearing to find it torn off somewhere. Then I saw it over my right shoulder and bent at a most unusual angle toward the left. Gingerly I reached around and pulled it around gently toward the front. It was numb and felt as though it were someone else's arm.

Carefully, I put my right hand inside my belt, and skated off the pond. With great difficulty I took my skates off and went home. I had gone skating without permission and I determined to do everything possible to hide that sin. My elbow now ached continuously, and the pain during the next three nights was excruciating. I didn't know until years later that my elbow had been broken that afternoon.

I had one more painful experience as a skater the following year. Skating in pairs, side by side, holding each other's hands crisscrossed seemed to be all of a sudden a rather grown-up and highly desirable thing to do, particularly with a girl.

The girl I favored was Rosemary Temple. She was about five feet and three inches tall, slenderly built, with blue eyes and long blonde hair. She was a quiet demure young lady who was never reprimanded at school, hardly ever raised her hand to volunteer, but always had the right answer when called upon by the teacher to answer any question, especially if the question had to do with mathematics.

I knew other boys liked Rosemary, and had noticed her turning down offers to skate with two or three different ones. Nevertheless, I was determined to ask her to skate, and in preparation for this momentous occasion, I dashed around and near her several times, showing off my best form and finally coming to a sudden stop, sending up a shower of splintered ice near her feet.

"Would you like to skate with me?" I asked, feeling an unusually heavy pounding in my chest.

"Yes," she said, extending her arms in the accepted crisscross fashion. As I took her hands, it appeared to me that I could feel a special warmth come through her gloves and into my gloves.

"Just don't go too fast," she warned as we began to skate toward the other end of the pond.

"Don't worry," I replied, as we began to pick up speed.
I was lightheaded with my newfound joy. Determined to impress her, I skated faster and faster.

"We're going too fast," she objected as it became apparent that we were reaching the end of the pond.

"Don't worry," I repeated, as I took two more strong strides and began to cut around to the left in a long sweeping curve.

Without warning my skates slipped out from under me, and in the same motion took Rosemary's feet out from under her. A hot wave of shame overcame me as I let go of her hands. Her sliding body ended up near the bank, while I went skimming off at a 30-degree angle from her. She was standing up, dusting off her snowsuit, when I reached her to see if she was all right.

"I'm sorry," I muttered with my head bowed low between my shoulders.

"You went too fast," she countered in a matter of fact tone, as she started to skate slowly toward our original starting point.

I skated off to the right and watched her slowly remove her skates and leave the pond. I resolved never to make a similar mistake again, and I never asked another girl to skate. Actually, Rosemary and I continued through the Moline Public Schools, and we were both graduated from the University of Illinois, but I never spoke to her again, although I did occasionally speak to her father Guy Temple. One conversation was especially significant.

CHAPTER 3

MONEY MAKING

In Moline, spring whispers its wistful promises in April. The fierce scowling winds of March give way to the zephyr breaths of warm waves undulating through the sun's soft rays; the air turns from the brittle crispness of winter to the rich silky softness of satin spring. The lilac bushes exude their fragrant essence around the most unexpected places. The lilies of the valley, the crocus, and the daffodils begin to poke their verdant fingers out of the warming soil. Now, too, the first robins hop around looking for beetles and worms.

Then most Moliners know that it is time to cast off the dark, heavy wrappings of winter, and open up their minds and bodies to the budding promises of spring. This Bacchanalian feeling is not all celebration and carousal; not in Moline. It is also the time to think about spring cleaning and summer jobs.

In all seasons, Moline is primarily a workingman's town. This seemed completely proper for me. I had witnessed nothing but a lifelong struggle of work in my family. My father always worked; first on the railroads in Texas, later in the beet fields of Montana and Iowa, next in the stone quarry in Moline, and he had finally completed the cycle by going to work for the DRI&NW. Most of the adult conversations I overheard were about work. I naturally became imbued with the work ethic, and it was only a question of waiting for the time when I, too, would begin to work.

My dad had always insisted that he didn't want me to do "camel" work such as he was doing. Most of all, he wanted me to do well in school so that I could get a good job such as that of a salesman in a store. I imagine that waiting on nice people inside of a clean building, while wearing good clothes, had the appeal for him of "the grass being greener on the other side of the fence."

Money was never the chief topic of conversation in our house, even when it might have been. After receiving a whole year's wages for our last job in the beet fields of Montana, we packed all of the belongings we could carry and went to Billings to catch the train that was to take us back to Texas. Here, Dad bought our tickets and divided the rest of our savings equally between him and Mother.

Since our train did not leave until the following day, we checked into a hotel and slept there that night. The following day, we got up and went to the train station, where we realized that Mother had left her half of the savings under the pillow in a little purse which she had carried into the hotel. When we returned to the hotel, the room had been cleaned, the bed had been made, and the purse had disappeared.

The loss seemed incalculable to me, and I feared that Dad would be very upset with Mother. He was not. Rather, he consoled her grief, and I'll always remember that his last words on the subject were, "We should never regret the loss of anything that more work can replace."

Work was one of the main topics of our family's conversation. We looked upon work as a provider of dignity and a sense of achievement. The nature of the work was not as important as the service it rendered. In rendering service, we felt important and fulfilled. This concept of work seemed to fit the spirit of those times in Moline, and it was easy for all of our family to fit in with that spirit.

I don't remember how I got my first two jobs. I do remember selling the Sunday edition of the *Chicago Tribune* in front of the First National Bank. Later, I became a junior magazine salesman for the Crowley Publishing Company. With a new magazine bag hung around my neck, I knocked on doors up and down the hilly streets of Moline offering subscriptions or single copies of *Liberty*, *Colliers*, *American*, and *Ladies' Home Journal*. I must have had some success selling magazines, but my experiences as a junior Crowley salesman came to an abrupt end as I almost became involved in what might have been a disastrous calamity.

One particularly pleasant Saturday morning, I told Mother that I was going out on my job. I put a full bag of magazines over my shoulder and sauntered slowly up 25th Street hill. Beginning on 7th Avenue where I thought the houses were nicer, I began to ring doorbells, and I was surprised to note how few people were answering them. Finally, a door was opened to me by one of my classmates who informed me, "My mother isn't home, but can you come and play in the basement with me for a while?"

"What's in your basement that we can play with?" I asked.

"Well, we've got a whole bunch of guns. My father used to be in the army, and maybe we can play with some of the ones that he brought home from Germany."

"O.K.," I said half-heartedly, "But I can't stay very long."

As we groped down the stairs, I noticed that the only light in the basement came from two little windows that were set into the top of the foundation. Gradually, our eyes got accustomed to the dimness. Sure enough, there were rifles and handguns displayed along one wall of what seemed to be a basement workshop.

My young friend's name was Dallas, and I knew that his father had recently been killed in an airplane accident at the Moline airport. Our teacher, Miss Straw, had told us about the accident, and had asked us to be especially considerate of Dallas' feelings when he should finally return to school. I thought it best not to mention what I knew about his father, and I followed him around as he told me that his father had been a captain in the American Expeditionary Force sent to France.

He began by pointing out some of the rifles, and telling me some story about each piece that he had obviously heard from his father. He seemed lost in his story telling, which became so long for me that I finally began to look for some other objects of interest. My eyes fell upon a brown leather holster with a revolver in it. I picked the holster up absentmindedly and slowly withdrew the blue-black shiny gun. As he continued to talk about the rifles on the wall, I put the revolver to the back of his head and drew the hammer back with my thumb. The gun's click made Dallas whirl around. I could see that he was rendered speechless with fright.

Finally he gasped, "It's loaded, you idiot!"

I had intended to say, "Stick 'em up," and tell him that I would have to be going. The gun looked very much like the toys with which we used to shoot rolled-up caps. I don't think I ever intended to pull the trigger, and now I was petrified that it would fire if I released the hammer. Fortunately, I held it away from both of us and slowly released the hammer.

We both breathed an infinite sigh of relief when the hammer was back in place without the expected explosion. I left the house with my mind full of all the terrible stories of how people have been killed with unloaded guns. For years afterward, I shuddered to think how my life might have been changed if I had unwittingly pulled the trigger and splattered Dallas's brains on the rifle display case of his dead father.

My second job might have set me on a commercial career! The

boxcar in which we lived was just a few steps away from the tool shed where the track workers gathered before and after work and sometimes during their lunch hour. Each of these men carried his lunch pail with a thermos bottle for coffee, but on one occasion two lunch pails had dropped off the motor car as the crew was on its way to East Moline. A quick inspection showed that the thermos bottles in both pails had broken and spilt coffee all over the rest of the contents, leaving nothing but a soggy mess in each pail.

At this time, Dad was the straw boss of this particular crew. He made arrangements to return home for lunch so he could bring these men to our boxcar. Dad often came home for lunch whenever the job happened to be near enough for him to do so.

Whenever Mother had to make food in a hurry, she used to cut up some pork steak into thin little pieces and fry them up in a large skillet until they were crispy brown. She would then turn this into a thick stew by adding water, cut green beans, and thinly sliced potatoes. She served this concoction to the three hungry men with the usual refried beans, rice, and warm tortillas.

Whether our lunch guests had been overcome by hunger, gratitude, or both, I'll never know. They were generous in the praise of Mother's culinary efforts, and they promised to buy tacos made out of this recipe if I would bring them to their work area during the noon hour. Naturally, I would know from my dad where they would be working on the following day. In the event that they might be working as far as Silvis, I could always take the street car for only a nickel each way, because the railroad tracks ran parallel to the street car tracks for as far as I knew.

The enterprise became an overnight success! Soon, all of the section hands on the Milwaukee Road became dependent on me to bring them their tacos for lunch, and within a week I had also begun to supply the workers of the Burlington Line with their noon meals.

The profits were greater than we had expected! Each morning by the time Henry Mengel opened his butcher shop on the corner of 25th Street and 5th Avenue, I was there buying a larger order of pork steak than I had bought the day before. My purchases of pinto beans had caused Steve Feeley to put in a special order for two 100-pound sacks. This grocer friend of ours could not restrain his curiosity as to what we were doing with all of the extra beans, flour, baking powder, and shortening that we were buying. When I told him, he seemed quizzical but glad that his business, too, was on the upswing. Little did we know that our business would dry up like the streets of Moline after a brief thunder shower on a hot day in July.

It was a hot day in July when I left Mother sweating over our hot stove preparing the largest load of tacos which I was to sell that noon. During the summer, sometimes the whole family would go down to the river bank to bathe and to cool off. Most of the time we took our baths in a large metal wash tub. First, however, we had to carry water in two 12-quart pails from a water valve the railroad owned about a block away from our boxcar. It took at least four trips to get enough water to bathe and rinse off. So, when it was warm enough, we just went to the river.

I told Mother that I was going to freshen up in the river, and that I would be right back. My return was much sooner than either one of us had expected.

I always knew that several factories along the river dumped all kinds of junk into the water's edge, and so I was usually careful where I entered and how I moved around once I got into the muddy stream. The heat was unusually sultry and oppressive. Nevertheless, after I stripped down to my shorts, I entered the water slowly and moved gingerly around as the mushy mud swallowed one foot after the other before sinking down into solid bottom.

I was just beginning to wash my face and chest when a lapping wave caused me to take a quick step to the left. Immediately I realized that I had stepped on the razor-sharp edge of a piece of sheet steel that had been half-buried in the muddy gunk. Even my teeth ground in dismay as I felt the entire sole of my left arch sliced inexorably to the bone. Panic stricken, I hobbled out to the bank where my worst fears were confirmed.

A horrible slash had parted the entire width of my foot. I could see the white bone smiling wickedly through the blood that came streaming out of many tiny places inside the cut. The wound was not painful just then. In terror and disbelief, I tied my shirt and my undershirt around the wound, and I hopped and skipped the block and a half home.

Mother was even more terrified than I had been when she saw my foot tied up with two blood-soaked rags. Quickly, I told her what had happened, and just as quickly, she carefully bathed my foot in our pail of drinking water. Then she took a clean sheet, tore off several strips and bandaged my foot carefully. It had now begun to ache with a steady, throbbing pain.

Every day, for many days to follow, she took the soiled bandages off, washed my foot carefully, and put on fresh bandages made from the same sheet. It never struck any of us that I should go to the doctor. We prayed and believed that everything would turn out all right. It did. Only the taco business died.

At the end of the summer, after my foot had recovered completely, I gave the taco business one more try. Before my accident, many of the workers had stopped bringing their lunches. They had become completely dependent on my regular deliveries. Once I stopped coming, and they kept going hungry, they all began bringing their own lunches again. Evidently, they understood that they could not trust an 11-year-old entrepreneur. Anyway, summer was about to end and school was about to begin.

In the early spring of 1928, I became "the foot-in-the-door" for an enterprising salesman for the L.B. Price Mercantile Company. He came to our boxcar with two large valises full of merchandise, which he asked permission to show. Later, I learned that his modus operandi was always the same. After he got into the house, he'd look for the nearest bed and proceed to display his wares, folded neatly and compactly over the entire surface of the bed, until he had succeeded in emptying both traveling bags. Then he would ask the prospective buyer what she liked most.

Most of his merchandise consisted of colorful bed spreads, curtains, and tablecloths. He was careful to arrange them in kaleidoscopic patterns. In those days, Mother hardly ever went to town, and I can't remember that she ever bought anything for the house. Most of her time was taken up with the routine of housekeeping and rearing her large brood of children. When she did have a few minutes to herself, she used to crochet doilies, curtains, and even one bedspread.

I knew that she was impressed with this man's array, and soon I found myself interpreting her Spanish to English and his English to Spanish. It all seemed very simple. For 50 cents or one dollar, you could buy any item, which he would leave right then and there; then, if the husband later agreed, pay for the rest of the cost, on time! Otherwise, he would simply return for the unused article and refund the down payment. Mother never bought anything from this, or any other, door-to-door salesman, but after he left, the three of us agreed that if I would take him wherever other Mexican families lived, he would pay me one dollar per day plus he would buy me lunch at some restaurant.

Since school was most important, Dad said that I could only go with this man on Saturdays when the weather was nice. He told me that his name was Bill Andrews, and he came for me as we had agreed.

I took him to many enclaves where there were Spanish speaking families. I took him to East Moline where the families were scattered all about. I took him to Silvis where the workers for the Silvis roundhouse and the Rock Island shops lived in a large cluster of company-provided housing close to their jobs. I took him to 1st Street down by the river. I took him to Jose Rivera's billiard parlor on 2nd Street and Railroad Avenue, and to Mrs. George Padakis' home just 2 blocks east.

Wherever I took him, we were never denied admittance to the house. Soon, he had me knocking indiscriminately on any door, whether I knew anything about the occupants or not. Everywhere we went, the people were very courteous, and I know that he left a lot of merchandise, "on time."

After the death of my first sister, Margaret, the King's Daughters Organization began to send out visiting nurses to inquire about our health, give us inoculations, and suggest procedures for obtaining better health. Actually, Margaret had died of pneumonia, and I doubt that anyone could have done anything to save her. Those were the days before penicillin and all the rest of the wonder drugs. When pneumonia was diagnosed, the doctor merely indicated a few suggestions to keep the patient comfortable and wait for eight days. My sister died quietly on the seventh day.

I knew that my parents had worried about her since her illness began, but I kept hoping and looking for her recovery. I used to come home for lunch each school day, and on the day she died I heard her crying weakly. While Mother fixed my lunch, I rocked her gently in her cradle until her sobbing ceased. Turning to Mother, who had come to look at her, I said, "She's finally gone to sleep."

"No, My Son," Mother answered softly, "She's dead."

I missed school that day for one of the few times in my life. We called the Furgie Funeral Home, had a funeral Mass at St. Mary's Church, and buried her in the Catholic cemetery in East Moline. We were all very sad, but the one who took it hardest of all was my dad. His life had really been fulfilled when his first daughter was born. His next child was my brother Daniel, and after him, we had another girl, whom Dad promptly named Margaret.

Different nurses continued to come to our boxcar home. One of these nurses began to take a special interest in me, perhaps because I was called upon to interpret her advice to my mother. She found out about my job with the L.B. Price Mercantile salesman, and she asked me whether I might like to have a more regular job. I told her that I certainly would, but that I wouldn't know where to try to get one.

"Well," she said. "I know a gentleman whose office is in the First National Bank building. His name is Mr. James Lardner, and he's a member of the Rock Island Arsenal Golf Club. Maybe he could get you a job as a caddy."

"What's a caddy?"

"A caddy carries the clubs for a golfer around the golf course. You're a strong boy, and I think you would like a job where you would be working in the fresh air and sunshine."

"Yes, that sounds pretty good to me."

"Here," she said. "I am going to write his name and the number of his office. If you'll go there some day after school, I'll ask him to give you a letter of recommendation and to tell you what else you must do. You should go during the first part of next week, because they do most of the hiring a week from next Saturday."

The very next day, I presented myself at the office of one James

F. Lardner Jr., Insurance Agency. He turned out to be a very nice youngish looking man. He asked me to sit down opposite his big desk while he asked me about my family and my interests. I told him about my school, my family, and my job experiences. Then he asked me to sit in the waiting room while he dictated a letter to his secretary.

Within a very short while, his secretary came out, handed me a sealed legal sized envelope addressed to Mrs. Copeman, Director of Caddies, Rock Island Arsenal Golf Club. Mr. Lardner then suggested that I should go to the entrance of the Arsenal Bridge at 8:00 a.m. the following Saturday, where I could hitchhike a ride to the golf club.

Upon the appointed spring day, I found myself in front of the bridge with approximately 40 other boys who had also learned that this was the day new caddies would be hired. I was somewhat surprised that I was the only one with a letter of recommendation. Some of the other boys had bicycles, but most of them would have to hitchhike rides from the workers or the golfers when they finally let us across the bridge exactly at 8:00 a.m.

Caddying at the Rock Island Arsenal remains one of the most satisfying and pleasant jobs in my memory, probably because I met so many quality people of various ranks. Mrs. Copeman was one such person. Even though she had a long line of applicants, she took time to read my letter of application. She asked me about my brief association with Jim Lardner, and predicted that I would become a fine caddy.

Soon thereafter she started calling me "Mex." I noticed that she had a nickname for most of her favorite caddies, coworkers, and even the club members. Of course she called several of them "Swede," one of them "Dane," and my classmate, Carl Hokanson, was called by a nickname which he seemed to have invented for himself, "Chink." In turn, Mrs. Copeman was universally referred to by players, caddies, and other employees as "Copie."

We used to receive a written assignment to caddy for a specific player from our caddymaster, Mr. Arndt. Then we went to the pro shop where Gus Flider handed us the proper golf bag. Gus did a variety of jobs for Thomas McQuarrie, the golf pro.

Gus was always pleasant and courteous to the caddies. He turned taciturn only when any Moline High School team was defeated. The event that held the greatest sports interest among Moliners in those days was the Quad Cities Football Championship, a round robin played among the four high schools of the area. I once asked him for the results of a game between Moline and Davenport which I knew he had attended. "Moline won second place," he replied with more of a feeling of pride than of bitterness.

Gus was generally as friendly as Thomas McQuarrie was aloof. Whether in giving a lesson or in casual conversation, he was always curt, polite, and properly professional. I didn't quite understand his impersonal approach either to his students or to us caddies. Since becoming a teacher, I better appreciate his position. Gus, Copie, Mr. Arndt, and all of the caddies understood that we were kind of day-to-day casual servants of the golfers, but Thomas McQuarrie was circumspectly trying to become more.

Copie was the real flywheel of the Rock Island Arsenal Golf Club. She was not only the real boss of the caddies, but she seemed to be at the helm of planning all club activities from the most casual match to the most elaborate and formal soiree.

I implied before that I was somewhat miffed when she first started to call me Mex, but I completely forgave her when I noticed the special warmth with which she treated me. I also noticed that although she seemed to be fully aware of her place in the social order of those times, she frequently greeted others with her own invented nicknames, and these included even some of the most prestigious members of the Rock Island Arsenal Golf Club.

Thomas McQuarrie, Golf Professional, circa 1932

I worked every day but one that that course was open for play between 1928 and 1934. I never questioned, and I guess nobody else did either, how a jurisdiction of the Federal Government of the United States could harbor within its boundaries the most selectively private enclave in all the Quad Cities area.

Among the Moline magnates that played golf there were Charles Deere Wiman, Burton F. Peek, Ben Butterworth, Frank Silloway, Herman Nelson, Willard L. Velie Jr., Frank G. Allen, and Harry C. Good.

Some professionals included James F. Lardner Jr. and Albert M. Crampton. The Doctors Louis and Henry Arp made the scene along with a few notables from other places such as Elmer Layden of the Four Horsemen from Notre Dame.

Colonel David M. King and a few Arsenal majors and captains also played occasionally as a kind of fringe benefit of their tours of duty.

I mention these persons because I caddied for all of them, and I feel that I got to know them quite well. Any golfer can witness to the fact that golf may not be much of a builder of character, but it certainly does reveal the human values and personal characteristics of the golfer.

I also mention them to show the social stratification that was quite obvious to me. For instance, none of Moline's public educators ever made that scene. L.A. Mahoney, E.P. Nutting, Charles R. Crakes, and George Seneff were household names, but they were either non-golfers, or they played elsewhere with the more plebian Moliners. I strongly suspect that it would have been unseemly at that time to have such lowly public servants dare to have either the time or the money or the boldness to disport themselves among a stratum of society to which they could never belong.

Gus Flider, Assistant to the Golf Professional, circa 1934

CHAPTER 4

CHARACTER BUILDING

The leaders of youth activities such as the Moline YMCA and the Boy Scouts of America never played golf at all! They never had the time. It appears that they worked endlessly to provide Moline youth with recreational and spiritual leadership because they had dedicated their lives to this kind of service in the same manner that the nuns and priests were supposed to dedicate themselves to their religious pursuits.

Hundreds of Moliners should long remember Norman L. MacDonald and J.M. "Morrie" Steffanson of the Moline YMCA. These two men really tried to involve all segments of Moline society into a common brotherhood. If a memorial is not raised to their names, it should certainly be raised to their efforts.

Dedication and compensation frequently seemed to work in opposite directions in Moline. The worker who, like my stepfather Ynez Bargas, labored for the same company during his entire adult life had precious little to show for his dedication upon retirement. The same was true of most workers, whether white or blue collar, whether working in the commercial or social areas.

Their reward seemed to be in having worked a long time and in having been good workers. My stepfather would come home with most of the skin peeling off his arms, legs, and chest. This was a reaction caused by the hot oil he used to clean the locomotives at the roundhouse for the Rock Island Railroad in Silvis. Yet, his only expressed wish as he scratched himself endlessly was that the itch would not get so bad as to keep him home from work on the following day.

There was no bitterness about this arrangement, either among the educated or the ignorant. The concept of work as the reason for living was generally unquestioned. It cut across ethnic, educational, and economic boundaries. John Deere himself encouraged the hiring of Swedes in his factories because, "These people are good workers, and they are skillful in working with steel."

My geology teacher at Augustana College, Dr. Fritiof M. Fryxell, in telling about the struggles of his wife's family, describes what some Swedish families endured: "Families sold everything to go to America. Most of them went to Moline, some to Geneseo and other nearby places. In Moline the immigrant families grouped together, several families living in a single home and all sleeping on the floors, many very poor. This is what your grandparents did with their little girl. As soon as they could they moved to a place of their own, a garret on Railroad Avenue furnished with secondhand material."

We moved to 518 Railroad Avenue in the winter of 1933. At that time, our neighbors on the corner of 5th Street and Railroad Avenue were of English extraction. We knew their last name was Enderton. Next to them lived Otto Wagner, who claimed to be German. Mary Dierecks and her husband were Belgians. We were next. Then came the Tertipes family, who were Greek. After them was the home of Sonny and Ines Otterstrom, who were Swedish.

And so it went, a veritable United Nations Organization before the idea had ever been born. The Frank Aguirres family lived on 55th Street when we lived on 25th Street, while the Jose Flores family lived on 1st Street. The only common denominator was that we all lived below the hill. The Fermin Guerrero family was the only Mexican family that I knew who lived as far south as 5th Avenue.

518 Railroad Avenue, circa 1965

Latin, French, Swedish, and German were the foreign languages taught at Moline High School. I went to St. Mary's Catholic Church most of the time. The Irish are generally credited with starting that parish. Occasionally, I went to Sacred Heart Church, which the Belgians were supposed to have founded.

I even attended another Catholic church on about 3rd Street and 9th Avenue. This was supposedly a Polish church, whose priest was Father Wojciechowski. He always asked the parishioners to call him "Father Watch-your-house-key." Of course, in those days, the ordinary language of the Mass was Latin for all the Catholic churches throughout the world. Usually, the churches could use the local vernacular for their sermons and announcements. In all of Moline's Catholic churches I never heard any language other than English, except for the mandated parts which were always in Latin.

If the promise of steady work was the beckoning force that attracted most of the people to Moline from diverse parts of the world, religion was the stabilizing force that gave character, value judgments, and strength to overcome the many adversities that occasionally befell even the most fortunate Moliners.

Even those without particular religious ties could find leadership and comfort in character building agencies such as the YMCA. How they found and retained men of the quality of Morrie Steffanson I'll never know. Actually, while I greatly admired Morrie, I also felt very sorry for him. He put forth so much time, effort, and patience in what appeared a truly thankless job.

He sacrificed his home life to take boys on trips from places as close as Camp Hauberg along the Mississippi River to as far away as Mexico City. He did nearly all of the chores on the jaunts. He was the truck driver and mechanic. He did all of the cooking and most of the cleanup. Finally, late in the evening, he would pick up his guitar and lead us in storytelling and in community singing. Many of us tested his patience and his perspicacity. Once when he was particularly busy trying to cook a big meal for about 30 starving boys, I asked him how he did it all. With a sly smile and a friendly twinkle in his eye, he replied, "By guess and by golly."

"How's that?" I inquired.

"I cook like I do most other things, by guess. And by golly, they generally turn out good."

Nowhere was Morrie sharper than as a discussion leader, and our discussions ran the gamut from boy-girl relations to world peace problems and back to race relations in our own country. He was the Hi-Y leader. The Hi-Y was composed of boys clubs from the high school that met at the YMCA. The seniors, juniors, sophomores, and the freshmen met in their own separate groups for discussions, swimming, athletics, and parties.

At one of the senior meetings, the discussion became a hot debate on race relations. As usual, the debate finally settled on the issue of inter-marriage and miscegenation. At that time, Morrie had a sister who was a student at Moline High School. I think it was John Sandberg who confronted him with the old, personal question, "How would you like to have your sister marry a negro?"

Without a moment's hesitation Morrie replied, "I would only hope that my sister would marry him not because he happens to be a negro, but rather because she loves him as an individual."

No more was said on that subject that day.

Morrie Steffanson was an indefatigable worker for justice and humanity. Everyone who only remotely knew about his efforts realized that he was overworked and underpaid. I often wondered how long he could continue to operate mostly on zeal and dedication. Finally, he left the YMCA and went into ministry.

~ ~ ~

I met many other persons whose mighty sermons reached me through their actions. I mentioned before how Frank DeJaeger used to bless me and hope that someday I might become a priest. Had he asked me to enter the seminary after he helped me out with my bicycle, I probably would have done it on the spot.

I had bought a new Excelsior bicycle in a shop on 4th Avenue and 14th Street. I was using this bike to get to my caddying job on the Arsenal, and I was making payments on it from my weekly wages. One day, I left this bike on its stand in the alley behind the shop while I went in to make a payment. I had heard a small grinding noise, but didn't think anything about it until I came back into the alley and saw my bike lying in the middle of the alley and reduced to a mashed and twisted wreck.

I noticed a truck speeding out of the alley and I assumed that it was a Consumers Sand & Gravel truck. I also assumed that it ran over my bike, but there was no way I could prove it, nor was there anything I could do about it. Tenderly, I picked up my wreck and carried it into the shop where the repairman confirmed my worst fears. There was no way to salvage that bike or any of its parts.

I got permission to leave the twisted wreck in the shop, and I started to walk home slowly and sadly. I imagined how a cowboy must feel when he has to shoot his injured mount, take off the saddle, and leave the beloved horse on the trail. I was feeling about as low as one can possibly feel when I came to DeJaeger's Hardware store. I looked into the doorway as Frank came toward me, ready to lock up for the evening.

He evidently read the worried concern on my face, and asked what was troubling me so much. Resignedly, I sobbed out my sad story. "You just wait while I call the Chief," he commanded.

I had no idea who "the Chief" was, or what Frank intended to do, but on the telephone he sounded more angry and upset than I had ever known him to be. Much later, I discovered that he had called Ben DeJaeger, Moline's Chief of Police, who incidentally happened to be Frank's brother. When he finally finished this telephone conversation, he told me to return to the bicycle shop on the following day. I did just that, and was completely overwhelmed when the owner of the shop presented me with a brand new Excelsior.

Many years later, a Ruth Clifton got a great deal of credit for the establishment of a young people's movement called the Teen Canteen. The central idea seemed to be that all that youth needed to keep them out of trouble was some place where they could entertain themselves with a minimum of adult supervision. RKO even made a film on this subject entitled *Are These Our Children?*

Moline's Canteen was named the Moline Youth Recreation Center, and when RKO made its movie on this subject and hired Ruth as a consultant, she proclaimed, "I speak for the boys and girls of Moline, Illinois." None of the real leaders of Moline's youth that I knew would have claimed such distinction.

I was a member of the YMCA, the Boy Scouts, and the Sea Scouts; and in all of these organizations I met many fine men and women who were truly dedicated to serving the youth of Moline.

I especially would like to mention a Mrs. Rank, who served basic and inexpensive meals during the lunch hour to students of Moline High School who could not afford to eat in the school cafeteria. She gave many a meal away free to the truly needy without fanfare or acknowledgment.

The priest of the Episcopalian church at the foot of 17th Street and 8th Avenue regularly opened up his parish house to a large group of high school boys who came to play chess, checkers, and to discuss a variety of problems with this kind and saintly man, Father Channing F. Savage. Their actions prove that "charity begins at home."

CHAPTER 5

DECISION

I also feel a debt of gratitude to Guy Temple. I knew that Guy ran the sporting goods store on 6th Avenue and 16th Street, because Coach Seneff used to send us to his store to be fitted in football shoes after we had made the football squad. I also knew that he was Rosemary's father, although I don't remember exactly just how I happened to know that.

Perhaps this resulted from another Moline characteristic. In Moline, almost everyone knew everyone else's business, as well as who was related to whom. It was even possible to guess how this relationship might affect any future business or social event. At this time, I had no idea that Guy knew anything about me, my family, or my dreams, and yet, this casual meeting which lasted less than 30 minutes has had a very profound effect on my life.

I had been caddying at the Rock Island Arsenal Golf Club, and I was hitchhiking a ride home when this big new car stopped in front of me. Its front door opened, and Guy said, "Hop in, Jack."

I wondered how he knew me by name. Was it from those brief moments of trying on football shoes? Had Rosemary told him about the time several years ago when I had caused her to take a bad spill on the ice? It certainly was not due to my exploits on the gridiron. Just before the last game in my junior year, I had broken my ankle in a practice scrimmage, and realizing that I would not get to play in my senior year, I had become a cheerleader. Now, I concluded that this was the activity by which he knew my name.

"Well!" He started. "I suppose that you're getting ready to go off to college."

"I'm thinking about it, sir." I answered meekly.

"Well, don't just think about it," he snapped back. "Think only that you are going to do it, and don't let anyone or anything stand in your way. Too much thinking about what you're going to do leads to procrastination, and procrastination leads to failure."

Then he went into a monologue supporting this philosophy for about 20 minutes. I can't remember any of his exact words or phrases, but his meaning was clear, and in that short period of time I was convinced that the "wishy-washy" concentrate much of their thoughts on the difficulties and impediments, while the resolute constantly search out the means to achievement.

When I finally got out of the car, I half mumbled, "Thank you, very much, sir. Thank you, for the ride, but mostly I thank you for your interest and your advice".

Ordinarily, I would have gotten out of Guy's car after leaving the Arsenal on 15th Street. On this day, he had driven me all the way to 518 Railroad Avenue where we had moved shortly after Dad lost his job on the Railroad in the summer of 1933.

The whole nation was then in the darkest period of the Great Depression. Actually, as long as Dad had a job, we were better off than most Moliners. Not only did we not have to pay rent and utilities, but Dad's wages loomed larger as the prices of all commodities sank lower and lower. Furthermore, my earnings during the caddying season nearly always equaled about one-third of my dad's monthly pay. Unfortunately, when Dad lost his job, we had to begin renting on his meager savings.

We rented an upstairs apartment in a dilapidated house on 1st

Street and 3rd Avenue. All of us shared a two-hole privy in the back yard. At that time, besides Mother, Dad, and me, we also had my brothers Tom, Leonard, Mike, Daniel, and my sister Margaret living in two small bedrooms with less space than we had in the boxcar. That situation was barely tolerable, and to make it worse, Dad could not find another job, and his savings ran out. It appeared that we could expect to be evicted soon.

Then, one day when I was walking to high school, I noticed that the house at 518 Railroad Avenue was empty. I stopped at the house next-door, and I found out that a classmate of mine, Steve Tertipes, lived there. Steve didn't seem to know much about that house, but his sister Olga told me that a Greek national owned the house. He was a single man who had returned to Greece with no immediate plans for his return, and so he had left the keys and the house in the care of a lawyer by the name of Fred Railsback, Sr.

One of my closest high school friends was Jack Railsback. We had both gone out for football, track, dramatics, and forensics. We had parts in the same play, *Tiger House*, as well as in the senior minstrels, but it never crossed my mind that Fred Sr. might be his father. I found this out when I went to his office to inquire about Mr. Apostel's empty house. I came right to the point. I told him that I'd like to rent the house, but that the only money I had was some $200 in school savings which were currently frozen by President Franklin Roosevelt's bank holiday.

Fred Railsback told me that he had heard about me from his son Jack, and that he had noticed me in cheerleading, Sea Scouts, and other extracurricular activities. Amazingly, he gave me the keys to the house, and told me that he just knew that I would pay the rent as soon as I could. He didn't ask me to sign any kind of agreement. He didn't ask to meet my father or my mother.

Actually, he never did meet my father. Shortly after we moved into that house, Dad contracted pneumonia, and he died within the week on February 18, 1934. I was graduated from Moline High School the following June.

So, in essence, I had become the head of the family consisting of Mother, my four younger brothers, and my two very young sisters. My baby sister Mary, was born shortly after Dad died. Nevertheless, my head was really spinning with old hopes and dreams.

I had always planned on going to college. Just how I was going to accomplish this really didn't concern me too much because I always thought that there was a lot of time to worry about that. Now, suddenly, after the string of devastating events, I became aware that there were very few days left before college began. The prospect of my saving $90 for my first semester's tuition at Augustana College seemed very, very dim, but I would not let my hopes come to an end.

This was almost the end of a long summer day. Many days then seemed endless to me. I looked toward the sun as it set slowly and quietly in the middle of the Mississippi. It seemed to want to quench its burning face in the tepid yellow, gently lapping waves. As a boiling caldron spreads steam over its gaping mouth, so too the Father of Waters, excited by the tremendous heat of the Midwestern sun, continued to send out huge rolling wave after wave of hot moisture-laden air. All Moliners know that this hot, sticky humidity continues long after the sun is finally lost in the depths of the river.

As I entered our little house, I hardly noticed that Mother and my brothers and sisters had been waiting for me so that we might all eat supper together. Mother uncovered the freshly made tortillas, and she put the pans of pinto beans, fried potatoes with eggs, and a bowl of steaming rice on the table. I said grace hurriedly and started to pass the food around to the rest. I must have eaten heartily, because I was always hungry after a long day's work.

Actually, I don't think that I tasted the food. My mind kept whirling around searching for ideas of how I could earn and save enough money to get started at Augustana College.

It took me hours to get to sleep that night. I wondered whether that sweaty, stifling heat served any good purpose. Did it cause the green tomato vines to become engorged with some kind of energy that ballooned out the proportions of its dangling fruit? Did it cause the green stalks of corn to crack as they stretched out toward the sky? How many other Moliners besides me were also turning endlessly on their sweat moistened sheets, gasping and hoping for the early arrival of the cooling dawn?

My overheated mind kept twisting and turning over all kinds of different thoughts until one clear idea crossed my mind. I would have to become the special caddy for the champion of the Men's Annual Golf Tournament at the Rock Island Arsenal. That was the only way that I could earn and save enough money to get a start at Augustana College.

With this problem solved, I sank into a deep, calm, and peaceful sleep.

CHAPTER 6

PAST IMPERFECT

There is some disagreement as to who really "founded" Moline. It is probably best to leave that question unsettled. Many Moliners would mention John Deere, but John Deere himself was attracted to Moline from Grand Detour, Illinois. His success in developing a kind of plow that became much in demand, in turn, attracted immigrants from all parts of Europe, from Mexico, and from other areas of the United States.

When I first became conscious of the "other" immigrants, it appeared that most of the Germans had settled in Davenport; most of the Belgians had settled in East Moline; and most of the Swedes had come to Moline. Among the laboring class, there were still some vestiges of foreign cultures such as clubs, languages, foods, holidays, etc. The general feeling among the young was that we might be living in a cosmopolitan society, but that we were all Americans. This feeling was a strongly rooted belief within me. I can never remember considering myself a foreigner even though I knew that until 1944, I was an illegal alien.

My parents were both illegal aliens, so were all of my relatives who had immigrated with us, and so too were all of the other Mexican immigrants that I knew in Moline. Each had his own story to tell, much like that of my geology professor, Dr. Fritiof

Fryxell. All seemed to have suffered before arriving in the United States, and many continued to suffer after settling down here. I only know of one person who willingly returned to Mexico for permanent residence there, after living in Moline. He was my second cousin, Dolores Cervantes. His father was my dad's Uncle Ramon, a younger brother to my grandfather, Vicente Cervantes.

Vicente Cervantes and my dad, Octaviano, first came to the United States in 1910. Their crossing of the border was legal in every respect. Among many other atypical characteristics, my grandfather Vicente was an inveterate adventurer and a pretty good violinist. He insisted that we didn't speak Spanish, but that we spoke Castilian. He addressed most adult men as "Don" and expected to be called "Don Vicente." I was permitted to call him "Papa Chente." He and my father roamed from Texas to Montana working in one place just long enough to get them to the next place. Finally, they must have become homesick, because they returned to La Piedad, Michoacán and El Ranchito, where they were joyfully reunited with their family.

In the next few years, Vicente's second wife died shortly after giving birth to a healthy Josemaria. Dad already had a half-sister, Jesús. Then my Dad was married to my mother, Guadalupe Ramos, who promptly gave him two sons, Jose Eduwigis (the author) and Eriberto. Now the easy Norteamericano money was long gone. The need to provide a basic livelihood for all of us became more difficult and incessant. Even La Revolución made everything more dangerous and uncertain.

Guadalupe was 14 years old when she married Octaviano. While she had known and liked Octaviano for a long time, her greatest hope was that her married status might avoid the certain confrontation that befell fathers of young girls each time the Villistas or the Carranzistas came shooting their way into taking the town. Actually, each guerilla troop would take everything they could carry, including all of the young girls they could manage and any young men they thought might help them to plunder and rape the countryside.

Soon, her fears increased with the thought that the next band of revolutionary bandits would impress her young husband. So, she did not object too much when her husband and his father started north once more. This trip would avoid his involvement with the revolution, and it would provide money for the needs of her growing sons. Meanwhile, Guadalupe went back home to live with her parents.

That trip turned out to be much shorter than anyone expected. On their first exchange of letters, Octaviano learned that Guadalupe had born him a third son, Tomas, and that the other two were seriously ill with dysentery. Eriberto died the day before the train bringing Vicente and Octaviano puffed to a stop outside La Piedad de Cavadas.

On the way to La Piedad, a ragtag cavalry troop of 15 men took Octaviano captive, suspecting him of being a Villista. The incriminating evidence consisted of a new pair of boots which he had bought in the United States just before returning to Mexico. All explanations fell on deaf ears. Vicente was brutally chased away from his son with threats of being shot on the spot. Then Octaviano was marched to the town square next to the church where he had been baptized, confirmed, and married. The sight he witnessed there was bone-chilling.

A pile of bayoneted bodies, some still quivering with an occasional jerk, were stacked against one side of a huge live oak tree. Over the lowest branch hung a lasso with a slip knot tied at the end. He beheld with increasing horror a file of about five men obviously awaiting their turn in terror-stricken resignation. As a Mariachi band struck up "Cielito Lindo," the first man in line had the rope slipped over his head and tightened below his arm pits.

Then, he was lifted off the ground and swung to be bayoneted once from the front by a waiting soldier, and again in the back by another soldier. Next, the rope was slackened off the mortally wounded victim by his two executioners so they could throw him upon the pile of bodies, and thereby prepare for the next in line. Now, Octaviano knew the fate that awaited him.

In a daze he stood until his turn came. He scarcely heard his accusers deny his plea of innocence to any revolutionary activity. He was called a liar as he repeated once more that he had just come home from El Norte.

Finally, when someone asked him for his last wish, he heard himself say in sullen resignation, "I would like to have the band play 'Las Golondrinas.'"

Octaviano crossed himself mechanically as the rope was tightened around his body and the band began to play, "Adonde van Las Golondrinas."

Suddenly the band stopped. The fiddle player came to the tree waving his bow in one hand and the violin in the other one. He was shouting, "Octaviano! Octaviano!"

It was Uncle Vidal followed by his brother, Vicente. There was quick corroboration of innocence and release for one about to be sacrificed to the hungers, hatreds, uncertainties, and fears sparked and fanned by a country deep in the icy grip of an incarnadine revolution.

Since they had been forcefully parted, Vicente had furtively followed his son. Ducking behind the long rock fences, behind bushes, trees, and buildings, he kept searching desperately for some weapon or means by which he could save his son. Again and again he thought of madly charging into the troop to attack them with his bare hands. Along the way he had picked up sticks and stones, only to drop them in dejected futility. Once in town he had quickly bought a long butcher knife from a street vendor near the church. With this weapon clutched firmly he had been moving closer and closer to the tree, when he recognized his brother Vidal among the musicians in the Mariachi band. His incredulous cry stopped the music, and shortly stopped the execution as well. Octaviano was free!

This last minute deliverance brought an end to the day's executions. The bodies were doused with kerosene and a public cremation took place. Now the church bells were rung, as some of the soldiers and many townspeople went in to kneel before the altar of the church that still bears the same name as the town. That name in English translates exactly as "The Mercy of (Bishop) Cavadas."

As Vicente and Octaviano knelt before that altar giving thanks for their merciful delivery, each, as though guided by a flash of mental telepathy, decided to move the whole family to Los Estados Unidos del Norte.

On the way home, they walked pensively along the bank of the Lerma River. Its slow moving dark stream now captured the fluffy white clouds like a huge mirror so that you could look either into the river or up to the sky and see the same picture that Goya would have loved to paint. The evening sun tinged everything with vermillion hues reminiscent of that afternoon's bloody scene.

"Even the sky seems angry, Mi Pelon," said my grandfather.

"Yes, but it's changing rapidly," replied his son. Then he added, "We should move just as quickly. We can no longer stay here. Another day will bring another band of brigands. They'll climb the church steeple, ring the bells, take over the town, and kill a few more helpless men. They'll scare everyone so they can take as much plunder as they can carry and as many women as they think they can manage. Then they'll skulk away into the forest to make way for the next band of rascals."

"You're right, Mi Pelon. We can never live here again, without becoming a part of them."

Arrangements for the migration were begun the very next day. Guadalupe's father, Pedro Ramos, gave her his best little cow. She quickly sold the cow, and all the rest of her possessions that they couldn't carry. She considered that she would have all she could do to carry the infant Tomas. First, Tomas would have to be baptized, and then Eriberto would have to be buried. Octaviano had few possessions to dispose of, but for Vicente things were much more complicated.

As soon as it was known that Vicente and Octaviano were leaving for the United States, many other family members wanted to go along. Of course, Vicente planned to take his younger children, Jesús and Josemaria. They had been cared for by his oldest daughter, Concha, since their mother died. However, Concha did not want to be parted from them. She had "mothered" them for so long that she prevailed upon her husband, Martin Mendoza, to rid themselves of their possessions so they could take their three daughters and become part of the exodus.

Now, her sister Cristina talked her husband Juan Trujillo into going along. This was easier because the couple was childless. However, when the youngest sister, Maria, now married to Calixtro Olivares, also wanted to join the caravan, Vicente almost exploded. He had never approved of Calixtro. He called him an irresponsible drunk, and claimed that he could not stand for the unhappiness he would bring his daughter Maria.

Later Maria and Calixtro went into Texas with their children; Maria, Antonio, and Gregorio. The families left in different groups by railroad at different times, but most of them unloaded at Nuevo Laredo. There were 19 others who arrived at that destination in the group that followed Vicente and Octaviano Cervantes.

Left to right: Jesús, Vicente, Josemaria (Joe), circa 1929

~ ~ ~

Laredo, Texas, could now be seen on the other side of the small, muddy stream misnamed El Rio Grande. All 22 of us sat around the station munching on the remains of our tacos, fruits, and cheese found at the bottom of our lunch baskets. We lingered around the station long after the rest of the passengers had left the area.

We could see both the Mexican customs building on our side, and the American immigration offices just on the other side of the bridge. A heated debate had gone on in the train among most of the adults in our group. Some wanted to go in legally through "La Inmigración," while others did not want to take the chance of being turned back. These latter few preferred to wade across the river.

As evening came, and there was still no decision, Mother brought up a question whose answer finally brought about the solution. During the debate, the question of the physical examination had been brought up rather furtively. Mother asked what this examination included. Vicente told her that a doctor would examine each person thoroughly. Promptly, Mother proclaimed that she would not disrobe for anyone. All the rest of the ladies agreed that they wouldn't submit to any physical examination either. Dad's reasonable assurances that all the doctors wanted to do was to exclude those with communicable diseases fell on deaf ears. So, the decision to wait until dark to wade across the stream was finally accepted by all.

Evidently, the same decision had been reached by many of the rest of the passengers who had embarked on that train on their journey to El Norte. Incidentally, we escaped getting our backs wet. Our family paid to be ferried to Laredo, Texas.

Mother remembers that we started from La Piedad on November 19, 1920. She says that the Vicente Cervantes that came with us was Dad's cousin. My grandfather and other members of the family came on another train. I have gleaned most of the information about our trip from Mother.

She has a remarkable memory for names, dates, and other insignificant details regarding members of the family, but she has always refused to discuss any significant details about her own personal life. I have, therefore, had to gather bits and pieces of information from my Aunt Concha and from her own sisters to put together the following mosaic.

Guadalupe Ramos was the oldest child of Pedro Ramos and Vicenta Sambrano de Ramos. Lupe (a diminutive of Guadalupe) was born on June 10, 1900. Evidently she was a happy, healthy child who enjoyed an active childhood on her parents' acreage. The Pedro Ramos family was never really poverty-stricken.

I used to call my grandmother "Mama-titi." She was a large, rawboned woman whose face mirrored some Indian traits. Her kindness and generosity were attested to by all who knew her, and Mother claims that she cried easily because she was very emotional.

I called my grandfather "Papa Pedro." He looked frail alongside my grandmother. He was just about her height, slightly-built with deep blue eyes, and a very fair complexion. He wore a well-trimmed mustache and a pointed beard somewhat reminiscent of the pictures of Miguel Cervantes de Saavedra.

These two had four other daughters that lived into adulthood. Somehow, they weathered some 19 miscarriages, the Mexican Revolution, and managed to live to a ripe old age. They lived close to these four daughters all of their lives. My youngest aunt, Teofila, was born 14 years after we came to the United States. That means that she is 19 years younger than I.

My Aunt Martina tells me that the Ramos and the Cervantes families have lived in and around La Piedad ever since she can remember. The other aunts agree that until recent years, all of the women and the older girls did their wash on the banks of the Lerma River. This was a great time for these ladies to socialize, learn the latest gossip, and make important plans. Often, the young men would gather on the other side of the river, and occasionally they would swim to where the girls were in order to tease them, or to arrange trysts with them.

My mother admits to knowing, liking, and wanting to marry my father. She insists that she wanted to get married because of the uncertainties and threats of the Revolution, but exactly how her marriage was planned and carried out was indicated to me only by my aunts on both sides of the family.

It appears that Dad and Mother made some rather elaborate plans to "run away." The event occurred at night and the meeting place was in some field which they both knew well. Mother had to save some pieces of meat from her supper so that she could keep the dogs quiet while she crawled out of her bed and sneaked out of the house.

Octaviano had only to meet her at the appointed place, and from there he took her to my Aunt Concha's house. On the following day, my dad and his father presented themselves before my Papa Pedro to ask for Mother's hand in marriage. This was an important formality that had to be followed exactly, so that all of the principals could present themselves together at the church and request a formal marriage ceremony.

Everything must have turned out all right, because my baptismal certificate says that I am, "The legitimate son of Guadalupe Ramos and Octaviano Cervantes." It even states that the sponsors for my baptism were Pedro Ramos and Vicenta Sambrano.

Mother remembers that when Dad left us in Mexico, he used

to send us money from the United States. She remembers that twice he sent her $100, but she also admits that she worried that he might find some other woman in his travels. All things considered, she was glad when we left La Piedad, together.

It took us three days and two nights of riding in a freight car equipped with long wooden benches before we arrived in Nuevo Laredo. After our ferry ride across the Rio Grande, we were taken by farm wagon to the train station where we boarded a train to San Antonio. From San Antonio our immediate family stopped at Marquez, Texas, where Dad got a job on the railroad. Others in our group went on to Palestine and to other areas in Texas.

In time, an economic depression caused a series of layoffs that left Dad and a few "negroes" working on that particular section gang. Dad felt uncomfortable, so he quit and found another job in Panhandle. My brother Leonard was born there on April 19, 1922.

I went to school with some older girls who used to come for me where we lived in the section housing tract. My name proved to be quite a stumbling block for them and for me. It continued to be troublesome until I changed it legally when I received my final citizenship papers on January 7, 1944. Even some 30 years later, two of my grown children, Elizabeth and Charles, had a terrible time identifying themselves to my aunts in Mexico. These aunts had helped mother with me during the first five years of my life, but they had never heard of John Ross Cervantes.

I was baptized Jose Eduwigis de la Concepcion Cervantes, but I don't think that anyone except the priest who baptized me knew that. My grandfather Vicente had the idea that all infants should be named according to the saint's name that appeared on the Irish Calendar of Saints. Consequently, that infant's name and birthday would always coincide with his saint's day. Eduwigis just happens to be the Spanish translation of the Polish Saint Hedwig, whose feast day was October 17. Most of my Mexican relatives knew me as Edubigen or Edubiges. But usually they just called me, "Vijen."

None of these names lasted long in the United States. Mother explains that the girls who first took me to school couldn't speak Spanish, so they called me, "Lubiken Jack." I can never recall being called any name other than Jack by my teachers and "Jackie" by my childhood friends. Evidently my parents must have picked up on this latter diminutive, because they have always called me, "Cocky." I guess that was as close as they could come to Jackie, and Mother still refers to me by that name. The Ross came about as an attempted translation of Mother's maiden name, Ramos. I only hope that my third son doesn't have to jump over all of these name hurdles. We baptized him, John Ross Cervantes, Jr.

When my Uncle Martin Mendoza died, we moved to Amarillo for a very brief time. Soon my recently widowed Aunt Concha and her children (Mercedes, Ubalda, Guadalupe, Rosario, and Martin Jr.), my grandfather Vicente with Dad's half-sister Jesús and his half-brother Josemaria, and our own family (Dad, Mother, myself, Tom, and Leonard) joined an "enganche" to Billings, Montana. Next, we were taken to beet fields near Worden and Huntley, but wherever we went, all of us lived in the same house, and all who were capable worked together in the beet fields. My cousin Ubalda and I usually stayed in the house to take care of the younger children.

After the topping was done, the farmer paid my grandfather a lump sum according to the total tonnage of beets harvested and the price paid per ton. Then my grandfather divided the money he had received among the three families. Even the wise Solomon could not have pleased all the workers. Dad was especially displeased because he felt that he was the most productive member of the work crew. Furthermore, he constantly chafed under the benevolent paternalism of my grandfather. As if to prove a point,

Dad got a job working on the railroad, and the rest had no earnings for the ensuing winter.

My brother Michael's birth on January 3, 1924 further complicated matters. Soon after Mike was baptized, Dad and Mother decided to leave Montana, and we went to join my Uncle Juan and my Aunt Christina in Texas. My dad worked on the railroad there once more, and then my aunt and uncle moved to the Midwest.

I've previously mentioned the fact that Dad and Juan Trujillo were always very good friends. It appears that when they were not chasing after us, we were chasing after them. Consequently, we soon ended up in the Midwest too. This time we went into the beet fields of Estherville, Iowa, where we topped beets for just one short season. Our next trip was just a short hop to Moline, Illinois. Here I was promptly enrolled in the 4th grade at Grant School.

Reproduction of the marriage certificate of Octaviano Cervantes and Guadalupe Ramos

Obtained September 10, 2004 in La Piedad, Michoacán. This marriage certificate is dated October 21, 1914. Author was born as Jose Eduwigis de la Concepcion Cervantes in La Piedad one year later, on October 17, 1915.

CHAPTER 7

LEARNING

The Moline Public Schools I knew ran a kind of mass production, survival-of-the-fittest program which seemed to be fashioned after the successful production methods of its factories. The grade schools consisted of the kindergarten through the seventh grade. The buildings for these grades were similarly constructed and equipped.

Those school buildings with more than one story had oval shaped, metal fire escapes down which the students and their teachers were supposed to slide to safety in the event of a fire. Occasionally we had fire drills during which some of the students were invariably hurt, and the teachers would never slide down the chutes, so eventually these fire escapes were all boarded up.

The teachers taught all of the subjects offered in each grade, but there were traveling specialists in music, art, and physical education that came around regularly to each room in order to help the classroom teacher with new ideas.

At the eighth grade, all public school students went to a common mid-school. It was called Central Grammar. This school was housed in a large brick building. It was three stories tall, and it had been topped off by several towers which made it look like a huge Roman fort. Some called it "The Castle."

Moline High School was located just a few steps east of Central Grammar. The freshmen, sophomore, junior, and senior classes were educated in a large three-story building made of red brick, and decorated with white stone trim. It was an imposing structure as far as I was concerned. I marveled that it had a full basketball court in its gymnasium with a running track around the top of the gym.

Moline High School, 1934

It also had a large auditorium with a full-scale stage and ample seating for all of its students. Here each one had an assigned seat to which to come daily for roll call. The student body was seated in sections according to grade level. The freshmen were located in the front rows of the first floor, while the seniors had the privilege of going up to the balcony. All students were seated in alphabetical order. I sat next to Margaret Castle for four years.

Just across 16th Street, the beautiful mansion of Frank G. Allen had been donated to the Moline Public Schools. While I was in high school, this building was used for home economics classes, and its grand ballroom was used for class parties. The basketball team used the nearly new Wharton Field House and the football team used Browning Field, both of which were located just north of 23rd Avenue at about 17th Street.

The classes for industrial arts were held in an old grade school complex on 17th Street and 9th Avenue. Here Mr. Forest H. Groover taught machine shop and Mr. Julian S. DuCray taught pattern making, cabinet making, and upholstery. He evidently also found time to coach the sophomores in basketball. His favorite and often spoken phrase was, "We do it in this department."

My high school yearbook, *The 1934 M*, shows pictures of 173 seniors, 306 juniors, 375 sophomores, and 175 "sub-sophomores." It also shows the pictures of 47 teachers, three administrators, one librarian, one study hall supervisor, and one hall supervisor. The hall supervisor was Archie Swanson, who had recently graduated from the University of Illinois with a B.S. degree.

Seven of the teachers held master's degrees, 27 held bachelor's degrees, and 13 teachers from music, art, home economics, and industrial arts held no academic degrees, but they had trained in music conservatories, art institutes, and other similarly qualifying institutions. The curricular and extracurricular programs offered were rich and varied.

I took the academic program including four years of English, four years of Latin, and four years of required physical education. I also took the college required courses in history, algebra, geometry, botany, and chemistry. The rest of my schedule was filled up with electives such as chorus, woodworking, etc.

ALDA CARLSON

A real "Fem" athlete, that describes "Agie". Always on the basketball teams and did a good job fighting for the class. Too bad we don't have a swimming team because she'd be a strong bidder on that also.

FRANCES CARLSON

Who said all girls are beautiful and dumb. Take a look at this picture and then dwell on the fact that she's valedictorian. All we can say is that there's exceptions to all rules.

F. W. CARLSON

Here's another lad to whom school is a lot of trouble. In spite of this, he protests that he is not lazy at heart. Willared claims that he'll show us that he can make good—some day.

MARIAN CARLSON

Girls, you've got to give Marian credit. She's one who really holds up your ideal of getting the last word in when there's an argument going on. Whether it's right or not is some accomplishment.

MARGARET CASTLE

Someone told us you wanted to get fat on olives. We have heard of better things to get fat on than olives. Whether you're going to be slim or otherwise, we will remember you as a pretty damsel in the operetta.

JACK CERVANTES

Old "Senator" sure blossomed out in his senior year and made himself known. Jack's a peach of a kid and took part in a good variety of activities. You could always count on him in a Pan American program.

MARY JANE CHILLBERG

"Chili" was a miss who will be missed in music activities. She did her music exercising in the Glee Club and made herself known in the operetta. It was evident also that she had outside interests—not music.

HOWARD COBERT

Howard used to sit in Literature class and scarcely say a word. But in civics, it was another story. He was always ready for a good argument on some current question.

CHRIS. CORELIS

Chris. was always in some kind of new trouble, but how could he help but be? You know—if not, think of that bunch of bosom pals—now it's clear. There's no further explanation needed.

JESS COWLEY

A very well-learned boy on the problems and questions of the day. Not very big, but he certainly can hold his own with anyone in an argument. That's a good trait for any fellow.

A. CARLSON   F. CARLSON   F. W. CARLSON   M. CARLSON   M. CASTLE   J. CERVANTES
J. CHILLBERG   H. COBERT   C. CORELIS   J. COWLEY   L. COX   M. DAVIS

• • • • and our financial status low, we • • • •

LENORA COX

"Beny" is very quiet but we finally found that her ambition is to be a nurse and her hobby is sewing. With two such fine accomplishments as these won't she make a fine wife for some man?

MARTHA JANE DAVIS

Martha Jane's ambition is to be a music teacher, and what a fine one she'd make. She has a beautiful mellow voice which is the envy of everyone who hears her. Of course, she has been in the glee club all the way through school.

Page 41 of *The 1934 M*. Find the Author.

Author's high school senior year portrait from *The 1934 M*

Now that I have retired after 35 years of teaching mostly at the junior and senior high school levels, I appreciate the fact that my high school education was a pretty good one, because I had such fine, dedicated teachers who were competent and well-prepared.

At this writing I have maintained regular communication by letters, telephone, and face-to-face visits with my senior English teacher for more than 50 years. Her name is Marjorie Adele Hendee.

Marjorie Hendee is a marvelous teacher and a great human being. She has lived by herself at 1031 25th Street for more than 50 years, but she has never been alone. Her house is filled with books, pictures, and other mementos given her by hundreds of her students who have continued to visit her long after she taught them.

Moline High School English Teachers, 1934

Left to right: Bertha Siemans, Marjorie Hendee, Adeline Kerns

She keeps scrapbooks full of newspaper clippings of her former students. Some quite controversial, like Louis Bellson, whose marriage to Pearl Bailey became a cause célèbre among Moliners for a little while. Some who always seemed to do all of the right things and were generally admired, like one of Moline's best tennis players, Kenneth Johnson. As an American prisoner in occupied Italy during World War II, he made a daring escape, and subsequently married Lt. J.G. Phyllis Armstrong, another well known Moliner.

Some of the news clippings were about Moliners made temporarily famous by unusual events, such as when Allen Lee Gordon became the "Human Bomb." Evidently he was found with an unexploded bomb in his body which could not be removed without detonating it and thus blowing him up. Eventually, the bomb was successfully removed because he later quipped, "It makes a fellow feel kind of funny to find he's been such a good boy all his life when he reads his obituary."

I once counted over 100 different names in just two of her bulging scrapbooks. I recognized most of the names. Alphabetically they would range from Anders to Zelnio. There were more boys than girls, and while I never saw her at any athletic event, the athletes had the fattest dossiers.

During one visit I asked her to name five students, other than myself, that she remembered best. Without hesitation she named Bill Hart, John Kalamolos, Malcolm Bosse, Janice Heinz, Dick Luchsinger, and Norma Dendooven Zelnio. I am quite certain that Bill Hart is her favorite of favorites. He has also kept in close communication with her even though Bill has moved from Moline.

When I first met Bill in the Moline High School Gymnasium, it crossed my mind that here, indeed, was the personification of the "tall, dark, and handsome" lover that most girls are supposed to dream about. Soon I discovered that there was a lot more to this young man than just his striking good looks. He was an outstanding football and basketball player as well as one of the kindest and most sensitive young men I have ever met. Miss Hendee seemed upset when Bill married his high school sweetheart shortly after graduation from high school. I think she felt that marriage had stifled his future.

Malcolm Bosse is Moline's best known novelist. He graduated from Moline High School in 1944, after which he joined the Merchant Marine and the army, entered Yale University from which he was graduated cum laude, received Phi Beta Kappa honors, and delivered the class poem.

Bosse's first novel, *The Journey of Tao Kim Nam*, was selected by the *Saturday Review of Literature* as one of the best novels of 1960.

About his high school days, Malcolm Bosse wrote, "Perhaps my single finest memory of Moline High School days is of being in Miss Barbara Garst's Shakespearean plays. Those were in the days when Jim Johnston played Hamlet and Macbeth, and I can still see Miss Garst marching around the stage braying, and snarling and cajoling all of us into finally seeing the beauty of great art."

Miss Hendee and Miss Garst were best of friends as well as colleagues in the English Department. In regard to both of them, Bosse wrote, "Miss Hendee and Miss Garst set me on this difficult path of writing. They were the best teachers I ever had — and that includes college and graduate school. They possessed enthusiasm, insight and dedication. If ever I do anything worthwhile it will be because of them."

I agree wholeheartedly in his evaluation of these two great teachers, and like Malcolm, I have not experienced anywhere near the same quality of teaching effectiveness from any of my college and university teachers.

Even the not-so-famous have written about Miss Hendee. The following article, written by Dorothy L. Bjurstrom, appeared in the Letter forum of the *Moline Daily Dispatch*, and was entitled "85 Years Young."

Dear Editor:

Congratulations to Miss Marjorie Hendee, one of Moline High School's outstanding long time teachers of yesteryear who, on March 15, was 85 years young. I'm sure she is enjoying the many cards and greetings from as many friends and former students as "the gang" could reach to let her know just how much we all appreciate the many little things she has done throughout her teaching career to make our lives happier. Favorite people always make for fond memories, and for many the old High School and some of the very special teachers like Marjorie Hendee bring back many delightful memories. Not only did she make her classes so very meaningful to her students, but she always was willing to help those new to our country who were having language problems, and her extra thoughtfulness to the boys in military service was something to witness. It was always a thrill to distribute the mail and to sort out the many letters Miss Hendee received during those war years from former students newly turned soldiers, now stationed all over the world, who took the time to write her, knowing their letters would be answered, bringing news of their beloved school life now left behind them.

Yes, Miss Hendee, your quick little smile and twinkling eyes shine as brightly in our memories today as they actually did a long time ago. Thank you for all that you mean to so many people. God bless you and keep you.

Evidently other teachers have made Miss Hendee an object lesson for their students. The following is the result of an interview conducted by one Tami Chumbley on January 3, 1974.

"Teaching has its rewards," stated Miss Marjorie Hendee, a former teacher at MHS.

Miss Hendee taught English at MHS for 35 years. She also taught at Blackhawk College, then named Community College, three nights a week.

Teaching has been her way of life for 43 years, first starting in a small country schoolhouse. After spending several years there, she went to Lisbon, Iowa where she was assistant principal for a year. Upper Iowa University was her next place of business where she was a professor for three years. In 1920, she came to Moline and continued her career at MHS. Ever since she came to Moline she has tutored many students and adults. Retiring didn't stop her career for she still tutors now during the week.

Teaching was never her ambition because she felt it had no "glamour" and only old maids went into that field. Her original ambition was to become an actress or a writer. She might be getting a taste of the latter one, for a friend of hers has asked her to help him write a book. Again stating, "Teaching has its rewards," Miss Hendee went on to say, "I enjoyed teaching because I got to know the backgrounds of many families."

Odd things are always happening in class rooms, and Miss Hendee remembered a few of them. ... A strange man visited her room one day and started answering her questions even when she ignored his raised hand. By the end of the period, "He was ready to get up and take over the class!" she recalled. Although he had not acquired a pass to be in the class she still allowed him to stay.

After the period was over she went to the office
and found a note warning the teachers of an insane
man who had escaped from the East Moline State
Hospital, that had been visiting classes at
United Township High School. "The note said he
was putting teachers out of business, so I knew
it was the same man who had attended my class."

Having lived in a small town during her younger
years, Miss Hendee said she had no regrets of
moving to Moline. She feels that it is a wonderful
town even though it has changed quite a bit since
she first arrived here.

I have never met Tami Chumbley, Malcolm Bosse, or Dorothy
Bjurstrom, yet I completely agree with what they say about Miss
Hendee. Probably even if all of her friends, students, and acquaintances were to describe her, even that composite would present a very incomplete picture.

Like an iceberg, the surface of her personality shines and glis-
tens reflecting many facets, but the real Marjorie Hendee has a
depth and volume that defies any kind of analysis. She is both
modern and old fashioned.

She has always dressed fashionably and kept up with most of
the latest home appliances, but she never learned to type or to
drive a car. She has always read voraciously and of course she
knows all of the classics, but she much prefers detective stories.

When I graduated from high school she presented me with a
copy of Marjorie Kinnan Rawlings' *Cross Creek*. Since then, we
hardly ever finish a letter or a conversation without referring to
books. Here is an example from one of her letters.

I have just finished reading 5 best sellers.
I found "Burr" by Gore Vidal and "Salamander"
boring but informational. I liked "The Turquoise

Mask" and "The First Deadly Sin." I am now on
"The Blue Knight," a fascinating story of California police life. Joseph Wambaugh was a police-
man and writes of it realistically. I am fasci-
nated by the events, but I don't like all that
modern obscene language. But under it all it is
a very humane and good piece of writing, I think.
I have been reading Agatha Christie like mad. I
think I have exhausted her 60 novels. I don't
think they are "cheap" because they contain
clever problems and are read by lawyers and
judges.

Miss Hendee is at the same time racially color blind and ethnic
conscious. She nearly always refers to "my negro student Ron,"
or to "my Greek Dr. Kalamolos." Still I doubt that either one of
them would take offense because she speaks so lovingly about
them. I know that she has split her Christmas dinner with Ron,
and that she seems ecstatic when Dr. Kalomolos comes to visit her.

I don't know how she refers to me, other than Jack. Once she
told me that I have the blackest eyes ever set into a human skull.
I notice, too, that she never refers to her Valdez neighbors as Mexicans. The following quotation from another one of her letters is
more insightful.

I am glad that you saw Mrs. Valdez on one of
your visits. She sure is tops! I love her more
every day. I probably won't feel like going anywhere for Xmas, but if I don't go to their home,
(after my 17 years of Xmases.) she will bring her
family, the Sandovals, and the Sabarets over
here, presents and all, and will bring me my dinner, so I shall try to go.

She then tells me how sorry she is for the misfortunes of two of her fellow teachers, Miss Siemans and Miss Wolf. The latter died of cancer and the former became blind and had to go to a nursing home. Then her letter continues.

```
    Here poor selfish me has everyone waiting on
her. Mrs. Valdez washes, irons, mends, alters all
of my clothes and cleans once a week. She gives
me two or three good shoulder massages a week.
She even does a little plumbing, opens jars, etc.
Then Mr. Hyning, a Belgian, who looks like a
gypsy, is the best yardman I've ever had. There
are the Griffiths who transport me to the grocery
store, to the doctor, shopping, to buy stamps,
cash checks, etc. Then there is my neighbor, a
teenager who shovels snow all around the block
and my steps every morning. My hair dresser will
come to the house if I want her, and I have 3
women and one man, 84, who take care of all my
social needs. Also, Phillip Grebs, a young doctor
(26) who takes me to dinner, to the bookstore,
etc. It is sheer luck personified!
```

I am sure that it isn't all good luck. She has given of her time to people like myself in terms of many, many hours. Mostly she has issued challenges, or given encouragement and ideas. Her wide circle of friends and admirers bears testimony to the deep appreciation we feel for her.

At one time, I became quite concerned about her finances because she had some very expensive hospital and doctor bills. When I expressed my concern as well as my willingness to help out, she wrote back giving me a detailed accounting of her financial condition which indicated that she had been very careful with her money and was in no immediate financial difficulty. She was even careful to explain that she had continued to tutor for such a long time, partly because she could use the money and because it qualified her for social security benefits, but also because she loved the work and the people that came to be tutored.

I've never seen Miss Hendee when she wasn't cheerful and considerate, yet since 1975, she has suffered great pain from arthritis. Since that time, she begs to be excused that her writing is not exactly what she would like it to be because:

```
    I can't sit at a table comfortably anymore. I
am in a lot of pain, especially in the neck and
shoulders. I guess one can stand a lot because
I've had this intense pain now for over a year.
It sure takes a lot out of me. I miss tutoring
terribly. I take codine and triple empirin about
3 times a night or I couldn't sleep.
```

Marjorie must have been a beautiful young girl and probably had a lot of suitors, but she never married. Maybe her great love for her job and her students was too much competition for any one man. Whenever I asked about her love life, she became a Mona Lisa and turned the conversation to her scholarly pursuits, to the care which she had to give to her aged mother, or even to her pleasure of rowing her own boat on Grays Lake.

She never implied that there wasn't any love life, or even that it wasn't any of my business. I rather got the impression that, in the first place I wouldn't really understand, and that in the final analysis, my imagination would probably bring me close enough to the truth.

In one of these moments, I asked her what one of her unachieved dreams might be, and she told me that she had always wanted to write a book. When I told her that I also had the same unfulfilled dream, we decided to collaborate on one. This, therefore, is that attempt. Miss Hendee has been giving me all kinds of ideas and suggestions. In the interview she gave Tami Chumbley,

I even recognized myself as the "friend of hers that has asked her to help him write a book." I gave her the first 40 pages a long time ago, but since then I have been most unproductive in spite of her unflagging interest and suggestions.

The teacher to whom I owe the greatest debt is one whom I never had as a student. Her name is Mary Josephine Holland. Before I delve into my association with this wonderful person, it's important that I try to explain what kept my hopes of gaining a college education alive from the mid-1920s through 1939.

Most important of all, both of my parents were convinced that a good education was worth all kinds of sacrifices. As long as they were together, school was my first obligation! Probably as the result of this feeling on their part, I tended to associate with peers who had similar wishes and objectives. That was not easy to do in a working man's town where more than 50 percent of all children somehow failed to graduate from high school. The majority of those who were graduated immediately went on the job market even when well qualified adults could find no employment.

I have indicated before that I always moved easily within the culture of my parents as well as within the culture of my schoolmates. I found it quite distressing to note that both cultures seemed to be obsessed with the notion that the main value of growing up was so that the young adult could go to work. Obviously, the sooner young people could find permanent work the better! My parents never subscribed to that theory, and for myself, I found it totally unacceptable.

Here, I would like to try to analyze my love of education. Probably it derives from the fact that I could read for as far back as I can remember. As a teacher I have heard all kinds of theories on dyslexia, reading readiness, etc. I have taken several courses on how to teach reading skills from some of the best known authorities on the subject, but just how anyone learns to read is still a complete mystery for me. I do know that my grandson Jimmy Atkinson knew all of the letters of the alphabet and could read all single digits when he was barely two years old. I often wonder how much the *Sesame Street* show on television taught him.

There was no television in my youth. My early reading teachers were my grandfather and my dad. Before I was nine years of age, they had me reading the great epic poems *La Cancion de Rolando, Genoveva de Brabante,* and *El Cid Campeador.* These were just adventure stories in Spanish for me, and it was quite a revelation when Miss Hendee made us memorize a long definition of the epic poem which begins, "The epic is the most majestic type of poetry. It is a long narrative whose subjects go far beyond the realm of individuals, etc." Examples of this type of poetry included *El Cid, La Chanson de Roland,* and *Genoveve de Brabante.* These were obviously the same stories I had read in Spanish some 10 years ago.

Dad even taught Mother how to read and write in Spanish. I remember with great pleasure what a warm and pleasant relationship they had. When Tom and I were very young, they'd spend long, lazy Saturday and Sunday afternoons picnicking in some park, flying homemade kites in some open field, or poring over some sheet of paper half-filled with numbers and letters. Strangely enough, I wrote all of the letters to Mother's relatives in Mexico since I was eight years old, and I still find myself doing that on occasion.

So, I can't remember just when or how I learned to read, nor can I remember just when or how I became obsessed with the idea of going to college. Dad and I had begun to form a best-of-pals relationship since I sang in our high school production of *The Pirates of Penzance* when I was a junior.

Dad and Mother loved to sing, and they would frequently harmonize on their favorite Mexican songs. At this time, I started to join them in singing, but more frequently I started to harmonize with my dad. Later, both Dad and I had speaking and singing parts in a Mexican Christmas production of *La Pastorela*, which Jose Rivera directed and presented in an old deserted shop along 3rd Avenue.

So, besides watching me in some dramatic and forensic pursuits in high school, he also was quite proud of my cheerleading activities during the football season. Going to these activities, talking endlessly about them, and planning for my future education strengthened our father-son relationship to a father-friend-son kind of rapport.

Even though he did not have a job, the economic picture in Moline seemed to be getting better, and he was beginning to follow some rather promising job leads. He was then about 41, and I felt that our future would become more secure as soon as he found work. We were now taking long walks, talking, singing, and even wrestling together.

I pinned him for the first time one Sunday afternoon. That evening he had the chills and felt feverish. The following day he didn't get out of bed, ate practically nothing, and complained of a back pain.

The next day, he seemed really out of sorts when I peeled an orange and gave it to him. He took one bite, gave it back saying, "Here, you eat it."

When he noticed that I held it in my hand he asked, "Are you afraid you'll be contaminated?"

"Not at all," I lied. Then I proceeded to eat the orange in huge bites.

Mother came into that tiny bedroom to look in on my dad. I don't know whether he was in delirium or in delusion, but he was obviously in great pain when he said to her, "Look at Jack. He could do something if he wanted to."

That evening I called in Dr. Lyon. He diagnosed pneumonia, and sent for an ambulance and had my dad put into a private room in the communicable disease section of the Moline Public Hospital. I only saw him alive just one more time. Then he was perfectly lucid.

We had just finished supper, when one of our neighbors, Inez Otterstrom came to tell us that Dad had the hospital call to ask that all of us should come to the hospital right away! We had no telephone. We quickly put on our coats and climbed up the long flight of stairs from 6th Avenue to the hospital. Here we found a nurse who conducted us to Dad's room. Then she left us alone with him.

I was gratified to note that Dad did not seem to be suffering. Quietly he asked us all to kneel around him, and I assumed that he wanted us to pray a rosary of thanksgiving which we always did nightly with my grandfather. It didn't even bother me when he said in Spanish, "This is my last blessing to you all."

Then he made the sign of the cross over us repeating in clear concise tones, "Lupita y mis hijos, los bendigo en el nombre del Padre, del Hijo, y del Espiritu Santo."

Then just as clearly he addressed me in English, "Jack, I want you to take the children home now. I want your mother to stay alone with me for a few moments, but she'll be home soon."

I did as he asked. On the way out I asked the nurse about his progress and she replied, "He has a 50-50 chance to survive."

This gave me my first twinge of concern, but I thought to myself that really he looked and acted quite normally.

We had barely taken our coats off in the house, when Mama came rushing in and whispered in perfect English, "My sons, your father is dead!"

~ ~ ~

I'm sure that his passing was a tremendous blow to my mother. Among a lot of other worries, she was expecting the arrival of my sister Mary within a couple months. I'm also sure that my brothers were sad because Mother was sad.

The one who probably felt the least sadness was my sister Margaret. While Dad probably loved her best of all, she was too young to understand our loss. Actually, his death contributed to her great friendship with Inez and Sonny Otterstrom. This childless couple virtually became her adopted parents until she was married.

As for me, my desolation became a dark and bottomless pit. I lived in a cold, blue, lonely netherworld for years to come. Poems like "Invictus" had a brand new meaning expressed just for me!

It didn't help any of us to have Dad's body brought from the funeral home to our tiny living room for an Irish-type wake. The neighbors and our Mexican friends came from all over Moline. Some came to commiserate, and others came to get drunk so they could better exhibit their sorrow. Some brought gifts of money, and others brought food and clothing. All of a sudden I was treated as the man of the house. I even began smoking that night to prove my coming of age.

The only gift I refused was a chicken brought by "Childo" Garcia. He was one of our town drunks. He also lived with Goya and her children without benefit of matrimony. I'm always amused that many in the "younger" generations believe that their generation invented immorality. They either have never read the Bible, or have never communicated openly with their parents and grandparents.

I felt especially sorry for the flower children of the 1960s who decried the virtuosity of their parents and referred to all of their antecedents as old fashioned and "mid-Victorian." In retrospect, it appears to me that "shacking up" was very rampant among the Mexican families I knew in Moline and, furthermore, it seemed to be socially tolerated. Anyway, I couldn't tolerate Childo because I knew that he had designs on my mother.

The next day we buried Dad in the same East Moline cemetery where we had buried my sister. Now I returned to my classes at Moline High School somewhat resentful that I had to miss tryouts for singing in the annual minstrel show. One popular song that was sung in that show had plaintive music and words that still come to mind when I think of Dad and that long, cold, lonely winter.

Throw another log on the fire.
Bring back all those memories I know.
I can't see the face of my loved one.
When the lights are burning low.

It took me more than two months before I could accept the fact that Dad would never return to take care of us. I used to have vivid dreams about him. Sometimes they were happy, when I heard his steps on the way up to check on me as I slept. Other dreams were lugubrious nightmares, such as when I dreamed that he had mistakenly been buried alive, and was then desperately trying to claw his way out of the coffin.

Then I'd vainly strain to wake up so I could go help him out of the frozen ground. Even in my sleep, I hated that part of the burial ceremony where each of us in the family had to take a handful of dirt and cast it on his coffin. The crucifix from the top of his coffin had been saved from burial and given to Mother. It still hangs on the wall of her bedroom.

Last Picture with Dad, 1933

Left to right: Margaret, Dad, Daniel, Mother; Author standing in rear

The first ray of sunlight returned to my heart with the arrival of my sister Mary. I had called the doctor when Mother was in labor, and after the child was born he gave me a plastic bag full of some jelly-like material and told me to bury the whole thing in the back yard. I did that and came back to see Mother holding this tiny, black-haired, red-faced creature that seemed so utterly helpless, that I wanted to hold her right away! Mother says that she was born two months prematurely.

I've held Mary a lot since then, and it was always a special joy for me. Sometimes, I used to flood our back yard during a particularly cold spell in order to create a small ice rink. That winter, whenever I felt sad and low, I'd put on my skates, and with her in my arms I'd whirl around and around on that crystal like surface until my arms and legs were weary and my spirits soared once more! Mary was born in April. I was graduated on June 1, 1934.

Mr. Charles R. Crakes was then principal of Moline High School, and he performed an interesting procedure which I've never seen again. I assume that he did the same thing with all candidates for graduation, but I can only speak factually about myself. He called me into his office one day where we talked about my ambitions.

Before he ended the interview, he called Mr. William F. Haberer, manager of the Export Department of Deere & Company. He made an appointment for me to see him during school time to discuss the possibilities of my finding employment in that department someday. It's proper to recall that those were the days of Franklin Roosevelt's newly proclaimed "Good Neighbor Policy" and that the Export Department was one of the few profitable departments in Deere's massive empire.

To say that I was overwhelmed by the grandeur and ostentation of the Export Department would be a considerable understatement. That department was housed in the second story of a smoke-stained red brick building which stood almost on the corner of 14th Street and 3rd Avenue. It looked shabby and unkempt from the outside, but the inside of Bill Haberer's office was large and handsomely appointed with a large mahogany desk in the center and a big brass spittoon on the floor.

Mr. Haberer was waiting for me as I was escorted in by his secretary. Almost immediately I felt overwhelmed because they were both large, massive, Teutonic-type persons, and because they both seemed so self-assured. Mr. Haberer introduced himself in a long monologue explaining his humble birth, and how his interest in philately had finally brought him to the heights of his current position.

He inquired briefly as to my background and ambition. I had to tell him that I honestly wasn't sure, but that I wanted to go to college and ultimately use my knowledge of two languages either in the foreign service or in some similar position. I thought that the interview had been proceeding quite amicably to that point, but my mentioning college seemed to prick him as though he had been shot by a blow gun.

"College," he said. "I never went to college. None of my office staff ever went to college. Oh, some of the secretaries went to business college, but none of my sales managers went to college, and neither did any of my foreign sales representatives."

Then he fairly lashed out at me, "I wouldn't hire you! You don't look like an American! I want all of my foreign representatives to look typically American!"

I could barely restrain myself from retorting that he looked more like Erich von Stroheim than Clark Gable. He might have sensed my discomfort as he looked down on his lily-white, pudgy hands with their newly manicured nails. I rose slowly from my chair and said, "I didn't come looking for a job because I am going to college first, but I do want to thank you for the time you've given me to express your views."

Five years later he sought me out for the position of translator and interpreter which I held until 1943. I then found out that his sales representative to Mexico was Ricardo Fisher and his representative to Argentina was Carlos Herdner, and that both of these men looked a lot more like me than they looked like Mr. Haberer.

At that time, I was caddying at every opportunity the weather and my school schedule permitted. Once school was out for summer vacation, I spent nearly every day at the Rock Island Arsenal Golf Club. The small amount of money still left in my school savings and that contributed by our neighbors when Dad died was almost gone. The income from my caddying job was enough for food, but I could build up no savings whatsoever.

In the late summer I finally decided that the family would have to go on relief so I could save money for college. Mother readily agreed. I even spoke to Father Barnes about that decision and about the possibility of his using his influence to help me get a job or a working scholarship at St. Ambrose College. He flatly refused, saying that I should shoulder my responsibilities in a manly way and continue to provide for my family as well as I could.

His attitude was most disappointing to me. I told him that if I could not go to a Catholic college like St. Ambrose, then I would enroll at Augustana, because it was within easy walking distance from our house. At this suggestion, Father Barnes erupted like Paricutin. He told me that Augustana was a Lutheran College, that they would require me to attend their chapel daily and that he expected that he would have to excommunicate me for attending Protestant services, because I would doubtlessly lose my faith.

The last two expectations did not materialize. Not only did my experience at Augie strengthen my faith, but I note that Roman Catholic services in America today are almost identical, from the opening hymns through Communion, as the Lutheran services I attended at Augie from 1934 to 1936.

That interview led me right to Augie! Among other thoughts I considered that if my faith was so weak that it couldn't stand comparison, maybe it wasn't the True Faith after all. Fortunately, at Augie I met another very fine man. His name was Dr. Arthur Anderson Wald, and he was the dean of admissions.

He told me that the Federal Government was going to put into effect a new NYA program of jobs in the community that would help college students defray their expenses. He assured me of such a grant, but warned that it would not be enough to pay for my tuition and books. I told him that I would find a way to meet all of my expenses. Evidently he believed me because in addition to my caddy's job, I soon started a boys' club with NYA funding. We called that club the West End Panthers.

Now my dream was beginning to unfold, but in the short remaining golf season, I still had to become the special caddy for the winner of the men's championship. The junior men's tournament started the following week, and I promptly became the special caddy for one of its most promising contenders. Unfortunately, I lost out.

On the very last hole of the qualifying round, my player hooked a long drive into the marshy rough made tougher by a clump of tall trees. I found the ball among the reedy weeds, but just before my player arrived to blast it out, I felt a bite like that of a fly or a mosquito on the fat part of my lower right leg. I slapped at it, scratched it, and tried to dismiss the itching as the foursome holed out.

It took less than 10 minutes for me to return my order to Copie, but when she saw me I could see her wince in disbelief. I knew that my leg had become swollen enough to make my pants leg tight, but I didn't realize that the rest of my body and face had now become bloated and grotesque. Quickly, Copie took me into the clubhouse and began to scream, "Is there a doctor in the house?"

There was. He took me to his office, gave me some medication, and watched me closely for about a half an hour. He cautioned me not to go back to work until the swelling had subsided completely. Then he sent me home by taxi. When I arrived, Mother did not recognize me until I spoke to her. I spent the whole next day in bed, and that was the only day of work I ever missed as a caddy, until I had to quit due to my age. At the Arsenal then, all caddies were retired at 18 years of age.

The golfer I admired most was a gentleman by the name of A.W. Mitchell. He appeared to be in his mid-50s, had a straight, almost military carriage, a nut-brown complexion, blue eyes, and a carefully trimmed moustache. He could easily have played the part of an aristocratic Englishman in the movies. He also had an identical twin brother and two beautiful daughters. His first name was Ardo, and his brother was Leon. They were both good golfers, but most caddies thought they were past their prime as competitors for the Arsenal Championship. I was overjoyed when Ardo asked me to be his special caddy for the tournament.

When the pairings were announced, his twin was in the opposite bracket with young Joe Von Maur. I felt that Ardo could win his bracket handily, and then defeat his twin in the final match. It didn't happen just that way. Ardo did win his bracket, but Joe Von Maur became his last opponent as the winner of the opposite bracket. I'm almost certain that Ardo's daughter Nonie, was then dating Joe Von Maur. At least, she was always in his gallery.

The final match between these two should have been filmed for Hollywood. Here was this older, gray-haired warrior pitted against the relentlessly long drives of his brash young opponent. Joe was probably in his early 20s, maybe just a little older than Nonie who watched each shot with eagerness and anxiety.

The golfing styles of these two opponents were in marked contrast. All of Ardo's shots were masterful but not dramatic. His drives and fairway woods were consistently long and straight. He pitched-and-ran all of his approach shots, and putted safely on both long and short puts. Joe's game was flamboyant and exciting. His drives screeched out to almost 300 yards. He pitched all of his approach shots, and rammed all of his puts. Yet, by the end of the 17th hole, the match was even.

The 18th hole on the Arsenal is a dogleg to the right with an out of bounds from the tee to about 225 yards away where the fairway begins to curve. The left-hand side of the fairway is ample, so that any reasonably straight drive of 200 yards or better, puts the golfer in an excellent position for an easy approach to the green on this par four hole. Ardo's drive was straight and true.

Then I noticed Nonie Mitchell in the gallery. She was red-eyed and weepy. Did Joe also notice her? I don't know. The next thing I saw was that Joe put his regular driver back into the bag and took out a bludgeon headed club which he used only when he was trying to get extra distance. I immediately read his thoughts. He was going to try to hit a long, high slicing drive that would clear the trees to the right, and maybe land on the green in one shot!

I knew he couldn't make it. The ball rose quickly and began careening like an eagle over the first clump of trees, but the very last and highest branch, snatched it and whipped it out of bounds. The match was over! In desperation, Joe hit another ball out of bounds, so that when he finally played the third drive safely, he was beaten.

Nonie Mitchell was now crying uncontrollably on the 18th green. She hugged her father first, and Joe later as Ardo holed out and Joe conceded the hole, the match, and the Men's Championship Trophy. I was also a winner. I had earned $45 for all of the tournament rounds, and Ardo Mitchell gave me a $30 tip. Now, my first semester at Augie was assured.

Ardo Mitchell, Arsenal Golf Club Men's Tournament Champion, 1934

CHAPTER 8

IDEALISM

When I went to Augie to register, pay my tuition, and get my green freshmen beanie, I felt overjoyed. At the same time, I felt out of place. All of the students appeared so well dressed. The girls were especially striking in their new colorful woolen skirts, soft fluffy sweaters, and tailored blazers. This was a new era in high fashion for the collegiate crowd. The era of the raccoon coats, flapper dresses, and wide bottom pants was all over. Stylish, comfortable, long dresses, or skirts and sweaters were in vogue for the coeds.

The men wore stylishly conservative three-piece suits or fine woolen slacks with great looking sweaters or jackets. I owned one six-year-old dingy, brown suit and a pair of dark blue slacks. I had neither a good sweater nor a nice jacket. That condition bothered me somewhat, but I knew I could learn in spite of it. What I couldn't forget was how Mother and my brothers and sisters would make it without my support.

Fortunately, I didn't have to face that right away, because Mother met Mary Josephine Holland. She was the principal of Ericsson School where the West End Panthers held their meetings and where my younger brothers, Leonard, Michael, and Daniel were going to school. Margaret was about to start in kindergarten when Mother went for her first PTA meeting of the fall. Maybe there weren't many parents at the meeting, or maybe it was just pure luck. Anyway, Mother must have told Miss Holland about me, because I had learned that she would like to meet me. I called her at her apartment in the LeClaire Hotel, and we arranged the first of many, many happy meetings there.

She shared a two-room apartment with her sister Rose. It was about on the 9th floor and it looked eastward over 5th Avenue and the Mississippi River. She thought she had a grand view, and I shared her feelings. Later, I was to learn that one of the strict requirements imposed upon the builders of the LeClaire Hotel by some of Moline's influential hilltop dwellers was that no building could stand higher than their homes on the bluff. I think most of John Deere's descendants had homes high away from the river's bank.

Her apartment was furnished adequately. The sisters shared a common bedroom and bath. The rest of the apartment consisted of a kitchenette, and living room combined. There was a hallway entrance between the bathroom and the kitchen which was rather dark until you reached the daylight that streamed into the living room from two large windows overlooking 19th Street.

I had never been past the foyer of the LeClaire Hotel and maybe I expected too much, but the apartment didn't really come up to my expectations. The showpiece of the entire place was a glassed-in cabinet displaying hundreds of empty bottles of all colors, sizes, and shapes. I soon learned that this bottle collection was Mary Josephine's only hobby.

She had prepared a fine meal for me, and she served it on her best china, using a frilly lace table cloth, fine linen napkins, sterling silver, and Waterford glasses. She was a good cook and the meal was very enjoyable. Then we got down to business.

I told her my whole story without embellishing any of the

facts. Lastly, I admitted frankly that I had entered Augustana on the blind hope that I could earn enough to pay for my college expenses, and that maybe the rest of the family might be better off on public relief rather than to be dependent on what I could contribute.

She listened carefully and did not interrupt me at all. Finally, as the evening's conversation came to an end, she told me that she would speak to her sister. In the hundreds of subsequent meetings held in that apartment between us, Rose Holland was never there. I didn't know it, but she was then the secretary of Moline's Illinois Emergency Relief Commission — or as the local citizens put it, she was the director of "welfare."

Soon, I found myself working for her as a caseworker for the lower west end of Moline. The duties of my job were simply to visit the welfare recipients and take their orders for coal, shoes, food, etc. I would then report my information to the welfare office in the King's Daughters Building on 3rd Avenue. With Rose Holland's final approval, the supplies were sent out to the needy. The only purchase orders handled by recipients were orders for shoes which were supplied by Moline's own merchants.

This job permitted our family, technically speaking, to stay off relief. I rather suspect that Josephine exerted some considerable pressure on her sister to let me have that job.

The biggest lesson I learned from this job was that all of the Moliners I met were proud people who found themselves temporarily unable to meet survival needs for their families. I never met any parasites on society. As an example, in our immediate block, all of the family breadwinners were out of work much more frequently than they were gainfully employed, yet only one family with 11 children applied for relief, and then this family accepted help for only one week.

In the entire west end of Moline, I could easily visit my whole case load once a week in the time I had leftover after my school attendance, study time, NYA job, and, soon after school started, practice time with the great Augustana College Choir under its renowned conductor, Henry Veld.

I tried out for the choir as a pledge duty imposed on me by my fraternity brother, Brynolf Lundholm. He was just "Beanie" to his brothers in the P.U.G. house, but he was Henry Veld's accompanist and assistant director. Membership in the Augustana College choir then was a special privilege. I had a terrible cold when I soloed for Mr. Veld, and I didn't think I had a chance to make it. How delighted I was to be invited to practice with the choir, and I was more surprised to be put into the first tenor section!

I reported to practice on a Sunday afternoon. Mr. Veld began by passing out the information on that year's concert tour. I was amazed to learn that in addition to an extensive tour of many large cities in the Midwest, we were also to broadcast a program from Radio City in New York, and to sing in Orchestra Hall in Chicago.

When announcements were completed, Mr. Veld began to warm up the choir with a vocalizing exercise. He had each of the eight sections (first and second basses, first and second tenors, first and second sopranos, and first and second altos) sing six notes using the syllables Da, Da, Da, Da, Da, Da. That sounded pretty childish to me, and then he said, "All together now!"

Only those who have sat in the midst of a group of 80 persons hitting six consecutive chords in the perfect harmony of a double quartet can really know what happened to me. The sheer power and beauty of those notes completely dissolved me. Tears streamed helplessly down my cheeks. My throat constricted into a huge knot, and for the first time I understood what Arthur Sullivan meant when he wrote "The Lost Chord."

I was jerked back to reality when Mr. Veld announced that on the concert tour, "Girls will wear long, formal black dresses with a white collar, and boys will wear tuxedos."

At the very next meeting with Miss Mary Josephine Holland I told her the good news and the bad news. There's no way that I can adequately express what this marvelous woman meant to me, but it will not be amiss to attempt to compare her with her sister.

Mary Josephine Holland was born June 16, 1873 in Rock Island, and her sister Rose was a couple of years younger. Their parents were Mr. and Mrs. Harrison H. Holland, pioneer settlers in the community. I know that Josephine (as all of her friends called her) attended Brown's Business College, and I believe Rose did too. Other than that, these two women were very different. They could easily have served as female counterparts for Don Quixote and Sancho Panza. Rose was the heavyset, practical realist; Josephine was the slender, dreamy-eyed idealist. Actually, they both ended up as administrators.

Rose was the secretary of the Moline Welfare Association, and Josephine became the principal of Irving and Ericsson schools. Rose was the prettier. Even in her later years she was blonde, buxom, and businesslike. Scandal never touched her even though she had many friends among the businessmen of Moline. Above all, she was carefully circumspect in all of her dealings, and I always felt she'd never take a chance for anyone or anything.

Josephine was dark haired, blue eyed, and intense. She intimated that she was engaged to be married when I first knew her, but I never knew to whom. She had loved her teaching job, and as a principal she saw herself as the protector and defender of her young teachers. Her allegiance to the United States of America and to her beloved Daughters of the American Revolution were actually the greatest loves of her life, but she didn't always agree with everything either agency did.

First and last, Josephine was a fighter for what she believed to be right. Religion had little if anything to do with that concept. I never knew either sister to attend church, but I'll always be grateful that Mary Josephine was on my side.

"I think that you should know that several of my friends don't think you should be educated above your family," she ventured on one occasion.

"Well, what do you think?" I asked her.

"I think if everyone followed out that idea, we would never have progressed beyond the Dark Ages. I have some doubts when I find myself in disagreement with persons I admire, but I can never believe that education has ever hurt anyone."

"I don't think it has hurt me so far, and I'm glad to be in complete agreement with you on that subject."

She shared my joy when I told her about the choir, and she sent me to Fitzgibbon's, where Mr. Fitzgibbon himself fitted me with one of his own tuxedos. Later, he provided me with a fine coat and a homburg to go with the tux. Occasionally, I had to return to the store for some item of much needed clothing which Mr. Fitzgibbon provided, and which I'm sure Miss Holland bought.

Next she sent me to her dentist, Dr. Ziegler. He examined and cleaned my teeth, and again I'm sure that Josephine paid for his services. Mr. Fitzgibbon later became the clothier to our entire family, and Dr. Ziegler became our family dentist, so I hope they were somewhat repaid for any largesse that may have been extended to me, but I'm sure that my real benefactor was Josephine Holland.

I was very happy that first year at Augie. I received fairly good grades in all of my classes except geology, where I was quite disappointed when I received a D from Dr. Fritiof Fryxell. I knew that he was nationally known as an outstanding geologist. I had great respect for his scholarliness, and I worked harder in that class than in any other class. I even think I learned more in that class than in any other class I took at Augie. Maybe the competition was just too great. The only other person in that class I knew well was another Moliner, Frank Byers. He went on to earn his Ph.D. in geololgy and eventually became a geologist for the Federal Government.

That summer I worked for the construction company that built the International Harvester factory in East Moline. My job consisted of digging 6-by-6-by-6-foot holes for the pylons which were used to anchor the foundation of that building. Since the structure was to be located near the river, mud and water kept filling the holes I dug. The heat, humidity, and mosquitoes made the job a real challenge. Most of the other workers doing the same work were from southern Illinois. They were tough and experienced workers, but I managed to hang on through the summer, even though I aggravated a small hernia into a good sized hydrocele.

I was more than glad to go back to Augie for my second year. Everything went fine for most of the first semester, but things started falling apart for me by Christmas. I got a job delivering Christmas mail, and that winter of 1936 turned out to be one of the worst winters on record. The snow would drift into piles several feet high and ensuing drizzles would freeze a top crust on the snow piles. Half of the time I was walking on top of the snow and half of the time I was breaking through the drifts all the way up to my waist. The cold stung and bit into me until I could barely feel my face, hands, and feet. Somehow, I finished the job, but the real problems were at home. My mother had found a boyfriend.

I don't know any more about the details of that romance than I know about the one with my father. I did start to notice that Mother was sometimes gone from the house, and that the children were left alone. When I inquired as to where she had been, she said that she had been visiting our neighbors the Ontiveros who lived on 5th Street and 4th Avenue.

We knew Josephine and John Ontiveros very well. They were slightly older than I was. They had married quite young and were raising a family. Meanwhile, they had taken John's mother in because her husband Sostenes Barrientos had been killed recently in some altercation where he would not come out of his house when commanded to do so by the police. They finally shot into the house and he was killed. So, it appeared to me perfectly proper for two widows to commiserate and support each other.

What I didn't know is that John also had a co-worker living with them. His name was Ynez Bargas, a laborer at the roundhouse of the Rock Island Railroad. In those days, that railroad had a shop train that picked up many of its workers at different points from Davenport to Silvis. They all arrived together for work in the morning, and after quitting time, the same train took them back toward their homes. John and Ynez rode the shop train every day. He was a bachelor of about 50 years of age, and my mother was 36.

I undoubtedly would have objected to any man as my mother's suitor, but when I found out about Ynez Bargas, I was livid with rage. I mulled over all of the disadvantages of age, lack of education, poor earning power, his 50 years of bachelorhood, his propensity for drinking; and every such thought heightened the heat of my anger and disapproval.

One evening I came home cold, tired, and hungry. Mother wasn't home. Mary wasn't even two. The rest of the kids were cross, cranky, hungry, and they had made a shambles of our poor little house. I fed them bread and butter sandwiches and sent them to bed. The longer I waited for Mother, the madder I got. As Bobby Burns put it so aptly, I kept, "Nursing my wrath to keep it warm."

When she finally came into the kitchen, I lit into her with all the verbal fury at my command. Nothing seemed to happen. I don't even know what I expected. In frustrated desperation I struck her with my open hand on the back of her left hand. She struck back with one word — "Dianche!" Then we were in each other's arms crying inconsolably.

She never left the kids alone again! Ynez and Mother were married soon afterwards. I doubted that any man of that age could tolerate living with seven growing stepchildren. Within a year, Mother gave birth to my half-sister Ramona.

As the years went by, I saw how wrong I had been about Ynez Bargas. He and Mother lived together for 41 years, until he died at the age of 91. All of us children of Octaviano Cervantes quickly learned to love and respect him. He worked untiringly to help each one of us in any way he could, and today even the grandchildren he knew miss his gentle goodness, his wry humor, and his great warm love for all.

As soon as Mother was married, Ynez Bargas moved into our house, and I moved out. I went to live in the P.U.G. fraternity house which was situated on the corner of 7th Avenue and 38th Street, right next to the Augustana College campus. When I came back to pick up a few things I had left behind, Mr. Bargas said to me in Spanish, "I understand your feelings — and in your place I'd probably do the same. I just want you to know that I could never take your place as head of this family, and that my only hope is that I can be helpful to everyone." It ended up being a curious kind of tradeoff.

In a sense I could have rationalized my abandoning the family. In reality, it would have been easier to cut off my left arm. We had played, grown up, suffered, dreamed, and prayed together. Although I felt that Ynez Bargas was sincere about who would remain as head of the family, I hoped that burden would soon be off my back and maybe out of my mind. Actually, the boys continued to hold a certain allegiance toward me for a long time, but the mantle of responsibility as to who made important decisions descended squarely on the shoulders of my mother.

When Mary Josephine Holland heard about Mother's marriage, she wanted to adopt me. She reasoned that in the event of her death, I could inherit whatever was left of her estate and that I would keep and cherish her precious bottle collection. I was never tempted to accept her loving offer. On the surface, it appeared quite ridiculous for a 63-year-old woman to adopt a 21-year-old son. In the second place, I could never ever isolate myself from my family or exclude them from my concerns.

Toward the end of my sophomore year at Augie, I decided to transfer to the University of Illinois. Miss Holland was completely in agreement with this plan. I reasoned with her that tuition was only one-third of the amount charged at Augie. Living expenses would probably be the same at either place. I could pick up another NYA job there, and maybe do enough odd jobs to meet the rest of my expenses.

There were other reasons for my desire to transfer. I don't know which were more important. Even though I had joined the self-styled best fraternity on campus, and even became its social chairman, I never felt totally at home at Augie. The people were too tall. Naturally, most of them were Swedish, but even my fraternity brother Harry Mead, a good Catholic and the captain of the basketball team, stood seven feet tall, barefoot.

As a social chairman I felt some prudery that was quite alien to me. Augie had written rules prohibiting social dancing and couples walking hand-in-hand on the campus. I certainly was never a "social butterfly," but I had attended all of the school dances and parties sponsored by Moline High School, plus some private and other agency parties such as those planned by the YMCA and the YWCA.

I started going to Mexican dances when I was only 13 years old. I don't know whether Mexican dances as they were held then would be the same as other dances, because whole families would gather at some hall, and these "socials" more resembled family reunions complete with orchestra. There was no such thing as couples dating to go to Mexican dances. I don't know whether this is the place to belabor the point.

Augie did permit folk dancing! Maybe the powers that be at Augie considered that social dancing implicitly held out the temptation to sin. All good dancers I've ever known differentiate the pleasure of keeping time to music from simply having the excuse to hang on tightly to a person of the opposite sex. Maybe Augustana's founding fathers did not want their future ministers to be corrupted in any way.

Augustana College had a Lutheran seminary just south of the regular campus in those days, and several of the young men I knew had come from other parts of the country in order to qualify for the ministry. Maybe that was part of the rationale for those regulations that I considered "old fashioned."

Finally, the curricular offerings at Augie were quite limited in those days. By this time, I had decided to prepare myself for a teaching certificate in the romance languages, but it was very clear to me that there was almost nothing I could take in this area beyond the first two years of French and Spanish. Even then, Dr. Beyer taught French, Spanish, and German, and I never could understand how any instructor could dare to try to teach students a language in which the teacher is not fluent himself.

Of course, in those days, and even today, those teachers who are not fluent in a language resort to teaching grammar and literature courses which they can safely conduct in English. I've always believed that that was a fraud and an injustice perpetrated on the hopeful learner.

There's an unfortunate mystique associated with most so called linguists and language teachers. Many believe that there are those who are born with a proclivity to speak in many tongues. One of my pet peeves is hearing from an otherwise credible person that someone they know "speaks seven languages." I have been active as a translator-interpreter for many years, but I've never met anyone who was truly bilingual. I've met many persons who knew useful phrases in several languages, but I have never met anyone who was really fluent in more than one language. The good Dr. Beyer was certainly fluent in English, but he didn't know much Spanish.

So, for all of these reasons, in the fall of 1936, I hitchhiked to Champaign, rented a room, and registered as a junior at the University of Illinois. In the process of renting a room, I experienced my first encounter with racial prejudice. In all candor I must admit that for many years I had heard my dad speak disparagingly about Los Hueros, and brag about Los Mexicanos, but I never noticed any particular truths in these snide remarks. Quite to the contrary, he frequently credited Los Bolillos with a lot of good characteristics, and he and my grandfather always called his youngest half-brother "El Huero."

Of course I was always aware that light complexion was definitely favored among the Mexicans we knew. Those who were white like the Aguirres, the Guerreros, the DeVernys, and the Albas were more frequently called upon as leaders of the Mexican community. Usually they also had the better jobs. Much later I discovered the same apparent discrimination in Mexico. My own skin color which was light brown in late spring, always turned into a deep dark reddish mahogany by fall.

As I walked around the streets of Champaign, I noticed that many homes had signs advertising ROOMS FOR RENT. I chose one that was closest to the campus on Green Street and rang the front bell. A man came to the door and I asked, "May I see the rooms you have for rent?"

He took a long searching look at me, and then asked, "Are you Jewish?"

"No," I answered. "I'm Mexican by birth."

"Well, come in! Come in! We do have some very nice rooms."

I ended up renting a room from this man, and we became rather good friends. Eventually, I joined the Cosmopolitan Fraternity and moved into their big frame house at 605 East Daniel Street. Before leaving, I reminded my friendly landlord about our first meeting and I asked, "Why did you ask me if I were Jewish?"

"We don't rent to Jews!"

"Why not?"

"Well, they're loud and pushy and demand all kinds of extra services!"

"Isn't that discrimination?"

"Sure, but we don't rent to women for mostly the same reasons. In addition to which, girls are always cooking in their rooms, and hanging their wash all over the bathroom."

"Well, that kind of discrimination may be justified, but..."

"But nothing, kid. If you learn anything in college, you'll learn to be more discriminate. Besides the unjust meaning you have in mind for this word, 'discriminate' also means to use good judgment! I'm sure your parents want you to be discriminate in the choice of your friends and your activities. Maybe that's why you're going to live in a fraternity house."

I couldn't answer him. Moline had been a place where discrimination had been a moot subject for me. I hardly ever joined in the few academic debates raised around the subject. I had never heard of the word "ghetto" — not even in my sociology class at Augie. The word "barrio" in Spanish simply meant neighborhood to me.

I've never been able to forget that brief repartee. It haunted me again and again when I heard and noticed that Jews had their own separate fraternities, that there was at least one Catholic sorority, and that there were no "negroes" in any of the athletic programs at Illinois.

I heard all kinds of explanations such as: that southern Illinois was below the Mason-Dixon Line; that traveling teams could not find accommodations for negroes; that southern colleges would not play against negroes; that Jews needed to live separately because of their dietary laws; that Catholics had special reasons to band together.

All of these rationalizations sounded pretty empty to me. Moline had seemed to have a melting pot type of society as far as I could see. Those who chose to associate by race, religion, etc. did so more through their own choice rather than because others had excluded them.

I do remember one instance in which I could have felt excluded, but I really didn't feel that way at all. Jack Railsback and I were walking past the old Stevens home when I made some remark about the Scottish Rite Cathedral. Jack told me that the DeMolays held their meetings there.

"What are the DeMolays?", I asked.

"Well, they're just a bunch of guys that get together and have a lot of fun. Do you want to join? I can recommend you!"

"What are the qualifications?"

"What do you mean?"

"Well, what do you have to be?"

"Nothing, just that you're not a Catholic."

"But, I am a Catholic."

"Well, I'm sure they'll take you anyway because my dad is a 32nd Degree Mason."

I didn't ask him any more questions. In those days Catholics were not supposed to go into churches that were not Catholic, much less into Protestant cathedrals. I had been quite curious about the nature of that large, imposing building. I never dreamed it had anything to do with religion. As soon as I found out what it represented, I knew that even though Jack was sincere in his invitation, I really had no desire to join.

What happened to me at Illinois was that I began to emerge from the cocoon of Moline's protective provincialism. Moline had served me as a nice warm insulator somewhat akin to a fetus' amniotic cavity. It was a great place to develop!

My sojourn at Champaign-Urbana was harsh but pleasant. Earning my room, board, and tuition was sometimes incompatible with regular school attendance and study. Often, the latter had to give way in order to satisfy the former. Several times I missed classes in order to take jobs washing dishes, delivering groceries, or other such available part-time pursuits. In spite of this persistent problem, my academic grades were good enough to earn my invitation to three scholarship honor societies, and several letters of commendation by the dean of the School of Education which were sent to my mother in Moline.

My main inspiration and support continued to come from Moline. During all of my three years at the university, I sent mother all of my laundry by parcel post in a brown cloth-covered cardboard box, and she returned it to me each week in the same way.

I wrote to Miss Holland every week and visited with her during every vacation period. She really provided me with the motivation to prepare for teaching, and in the spring of 1938, I received a teaching certificate which qualified me to teach French and Spanish in the 11th and 12th grades of high school. I never used that certificate. I worked for the Moline YMCA that summer, and by fall, Miss Holland and I decided that I should return to Illinois for my master's degree.

Actually, I would gladly have started teaching then, but there were no teaching jobs available. Even experienced teachers couldn't find work. There was still a considerable financial depression throughout the country. Relatively speaking, tenured teachers enjoyed the best wages and working conditions in the entire history of American education, and no able bodied teacher was leaving the job willingly. We both agreed that my chances of getting a teaching position with some hopes for advancement would be greatly enhanced if I had a higher degree.

I was very happy to go back to the University of Illinois. The only things I missed at Champaign-Urbana were my family, Miss Holland, the Mississippi River, and the lake at Riverside Park. The only evidence of natural water at Illinois was a dry creek bed, aptly called the Bone Creek, and Crystal Lake, which my French professor delighted in denigrating because, "It is neither crystal nor a lake."

The pursuit of knowledge and the comradery with so many brilliant minds both young and old provided me with a wildly sweet intoxicant, and I really was "hooked on the academic life!" I continued to do well in my studies, and began to dream of earning a Ph.D. when a gaping hole developed in my plans. I lost my NYA job in the library because of my alien status.

Just exactly how I qualified for that program in the first place, I don't quite know. I really did enjoy the varied jobs I held under the funding at the university library. All of a sudden, I had to determine how I was to make up for that loss of income.

Again, Miss Holland came to my rescue. She co-signed with me for educational loans with the Mary Little Deere Chapter of the DAR, and with the Moline High School Student Loan Fund.

She solicited the loans on my behalf, and all I had to do was sign and spend the money. Repayment eventually became something else, but these loans did make it possible to receive my M.A. in romance languages. With my B.S. in education, a valid teaching certificate, and an M.A. in hand, I returned to the beet fields for the third time since leaving Montana.

While I was away at the university, alternately suffering and having the time of my life, my family's financial condition had deteriorated to a dangerously low level. Ynez Bargas never earned more than the lowest laborer's wages. He tried to compensate by planting a huge garden along the railroad property right of way. Mother cooked or canned all of the produce that she possibly could use, but there were other factors at work that nullified their efforts.

The family of seven children was growing. Now it required more food, shoes, clothing, and many other expensive things. When I received my first degree, my brother Tom was 18 years old, but he was more of a hindrance than a help. Things got so bad that Mother was topping onions in Bettendorf when she finally decided to take all seven kids to the beet fields and leave Ynez in Moline to take care of the house, his garden, and his job.

The beet fields didn't help much! Mother had contracted to thin several acres of beet plants in northern Iowa when she and Mary came to Champaign by bus to see me graduate. I learned about her contract. It simply provided that no payment for labor was due until the beet fields had been properly thinned. Mother had to do all of the cooking, washing, and the rest of the household chores. Additionally, she had to be in the fields leading my brothers and doing the major part of the work. Tom frequently left the group to hitchhike or hop trains back to Moline to go to the Mexican dances. Leonard was then 16, Mike was 14, and Daniel was 10. Somebody must have had to stay home to watch the girls, because Margaret was eight, Mary was four, and Ramona wasn't even two years old.

Almost as soon as I took off my cap and gown, I decided that I must go back to Iowa to help Mother finish her contract. The only extra pleasure I permitted myself was to give Mother and Mary a quick tour of the university. It was really a kind of emotional farewell for me, too. I didn't realize then that I'd be returning in the fall. The highlight of the tour was letting Mary walk around on top of the highest walls of Memorial Stadium. After all, the *Illio* yearbook of 1938 had been dedicated to head football coach Robert C. Zuppke. Then we came back to earth!

Within a couple of days, I found myself bent over the endless rows of green sugarbeet plants with a short-handled hoe in my hand. The boys seemed to be glad to have my help, and we finished the job within a few days. Pay day was a staggering disappointment. Our total earnings were insufficient to pay for our bus fare back to Moline. What a quandary! Tom and I wandered into the small town to buy some groceries, and we ended up buying a 1929 Ford Model A sedan. This purchase created two more problems. One, we were out of groceries, and two, we were out of money.

So, we decided to visit a man whom the family had met earlier. He was a Mexican who was a permanent resident of the community, and evidently he had been instrumental in getting the family the beet thinning job in the first place. When he found out about our predicament, he put a pot of coffee to brew on the stove, and we made a meal of bread and coffee.

Then I asked him for a loan with which to buy a tankful of gas. I offered as security the last remaining memento from my dad — his gold-cased Elgin railroad watch. It had been our family's most treasured possession. I'm almost sure that the amount of the loan was one dollar. I never did redeem the watch. But we did manage to drive to Moline, flat broke, hungry, and the proud possessors of our first automobile.

The next sugarbeet experience was sweet and sour. I had taken the Ford to Champaign and parked it next to the fraternity house, because as long as it was in Moline, Tom would find ways to wheedle money out of Mother or Ynez so that he could go joy-riding in the car. The day I received my master's degree, I was so flat broke that I had determined to bid each of my fraternity brothers goodby and stay in that house until they were all gone.

Then, I intended to go around looking for a job so that I could earn enough to eat and buy gas for the drive back to Moline. My roommate, George Hamilton, was just leaving with his parents when the mail arrived. He handed me a letter from Miss Holland. It was a congratulatory card for the completion of my second degree, plus a $10 bill as a gift. Joy reigned supreme! I happily drove back to Moline to discover that Mother and the children had gone back to the beet fields once more. This time they were in Wisconsin.

Ynez and I agreed that that was another wild goose chase! So, I got a little more money from him and drove to a lonely Wisconsin farm where, late at night, I found them all huddled up around a kerosene lamp. They had been staying in an old, rickety abandoned house without any furniture whatsoever. They had used orange crates and boxes for chairs and a table, and they had evidently been sleeping on the floor. I took Mother, Daniel, Margaret, Mary, and Ramona back to Moline. The older boys remained to pick up their wages, and they came back to Moline on the bus with little to show for their troubles.

This wrote the death knell to any further educational dreams I might have had. Not only was I in debt to the Moline High School Loan Fund, the Daughters of the American Revolution, the YMCA, and Miss Holland, but it was plain to see that Ynez was way over his head in debt too. He had borrowed as much as he could from the Rock Island Employees Credit Union.

My heart went out in sympathy to this kindly man as I watched him toothlessly gum his tortillas and beans. In order to provide for my brothers and sisters, he had denied himself the luxury of a set of dentures and a pair of much needed glasses. I remembered Father Barnes' advice to shoulder my responsibilities, and I decided that I had abandoned my family long enough.

Home from Iowa's beet fields, 1938

Left to right: Daniel, Margaret, Ramona, Mary

Almost immediately thereafter, I got a job in the offices of the John Deere Wagon Works, situated right across 3rd Avenue, only about three blocks from our house. More than likely, Mary Josephine Holland had something to do with that, too. We had talked endlessly about America being the land of opportunity, and about

how Moline held up this example. One of her favorite success stories was about a Jewish immigrant from Russia by the name of
Max Sklovsky. He became the manager of the Engineering Department at Deere & Company.

His son, I was told by Miss Holland, changed his name to
Maxson, because he was Max's son. She didn't quite approve of
that change because she said, "We're all descendants of immigrant families and we should all contribute our talents to what
made this Country great. What's gained by changing our names
or our faces?"

Nevertheless, she did approve of Mr. Maxson's rise to become
manager of the Moline Wagon Works, where I started to work
with Deere & Company.

I never did like Mr. Maxson. I kept telling myself that ethnicity
had nothing to do with it. That he was just a smooth sneaky ma-
nipulator, but I couldn't help feeling that the word "Judio" took a
new meaning for me because of his apparent hypocrisy.

Incidentally, I had always heard that word "Judio" used many
times by my Spanish speaking friends and neighbors. I didn't
know that in all of the Spanish speaking countries it's a widely
used and abusive epithet. Anyway, this man's oily, unctuous
manner and his obvious favoritism of the few Jewish workers in
that office really turned me against him, so that mentally I found
myself calling him "Judio."

So, I was very happy to be called into the Export Department
to work for Mr. Haberer. He made no bones about his ethnic pref-
erences. Actually, he became very kind and generous toward me.
He seemed to understand that the job of translator-interpreter required some very special and rare skills. He gave me a lot of lee-
way as to the hours and the conditions of my work. He invited me
to his home many times. Once, I commented about his gardening
efforts and offered to help him. He gladly accepted, and we

worked on his gardening together. I enjoyed it, but he insisted on paying and feeding me whenever I helped.

I continued to be very happy with my work at the Export Department, I met some outstanding men and women who worked there, but none was finer than Mr. Bruce King, Sr., father to my classmate and captain of Moline High School's football team in 1934, Reinhardt King. I think I did a very creditable job there.

When I left Deere & Company, my immediate superior, Mr. Louis Ostrom, got a whole file of my translations together for me. One was a copy of my translation into Spanish of the John Deere catalog. I reviewed these translations several times later, and I was always proud of that work. The year before John Deere's vice president Bud Lundahl died, I turned the entire file over to him and suggested that he give it to Deere & Company's archivist. I hope he did! I think it marks a period of practical good neighbor relations between a gigantic American manufacturer and its prospective Latin American clients.

Soon after I started working at Deere & Company, I bought Ynez a set of dentures and a pair of safety-type bifocal glasses. He was most appreciative. However, we were all still in a very deep financial hole. Even my Ford Model A seemed on its last legs, so I sold it for $10 and bought a '37 Chevrolet, on time. Then, I practically gave up all hope of getting a real teaching job because my salary at Deere & Company was better than any starting teachers' salary, and because most states demanded American citizenship of its public school teachers.

In addition to my job with Deere & Company, I also taught night school classes in French and Spanish at the YMCA in Moline and in Davenport. I found these classes to be very satisfying because I met so many interesting people. Many names of those students now escape my memory, but I could never forget Dr. Clarence S. Costigan or Mr. Carrol E. Hicks.

I began teaching evenings in the Moline YMCA in the fall of 1939. At that time, my brother Tom became seriously ill with inflammatory rheumatism. His condition went from bad to worse. Finally, Dr. Dondanville said he could do no more for Tom, and that we should just make him as comfortable as possible and let him die at home.

All of the trauma of my dad's death came flooding back into the recesses of my mind. It was even tougher in a sense to accept Tom's possible death because he was on the threshold of adulthood. My face must have mirrored all of my sadness and concern while teaching, because Dr. Costigan stayed after class one evening to inquire about my feelings. I knew that he was a newly graduated medical doctor from the University of Illinois, and I also knew that he was in the process of establishing his practice in Moline. I eagerly told him all about Tom, and asked him to come to our house to see what he could do for him.

"I can't do that Jack," he said.

"Why not?" I asked disappointedly.

"He's another doctor's patient, and it would be unethical for me to attempt to treat him without his consent."

"But he's already given up on Tom."

"Well, if you're sure of that, let me call him to see whether he will allow me to enter into the case."

Dr. Costigan and I arrived at Tom's bedside at the same time. After a cursory examination, Dr. Costigan had Tom moved by ambulance to the Moline Public Hospital where he stayed for more than three weeks. When he was well enough to go home I asked the doctor what the prognosis was for Tom's full recovery. The answer was both good and bad.

"Tom's heart is irreparably damaged."

"Well, what can we do to help him?" I asked.

"There are two schools of thought on that," he said pensively.

"He can stay in bed and become an invalid. Maybe, he'll live a long time and maybe he won't. On the other hand, you can let him resume as much activity as he can do, and maybe he'll drop dead, and maybe he'll live for a long time. If he were my brother, I'd try the latter course."

That is exactly what we did! More than likely, Tom would have done that anyway. He lived to be 50 years of age, married his childhood sweetheart, fathered 12 children, and died suddenly of a heart attack. He was in some local bar drinking a glass of beer and completing the narration of a joke when he crumpled slowly to the ground and died with a smile on his face.

Dr. Costigan continued to be our family doctor for a full 40 years. He sutured up the hernia that caused my 4-F status during the draft for World War II military service. He took care of my son, Joseph, when he became so feverish that he lost consciousness during a summer vacation when we had gone back to Moline. He continued to take care of Mother and the rest of the family until each of my brothers and sisters left home.

Finally, he told Mother that his eyesight had failed to the point where he could no longer take care of her. Always he kept up his interest in the Spanish language, and he made several visits to Mexico because of his interest in the language and its people.

Carrol E. Hicks was a florist from Carbon Cliff, Illinois. He was one of my most faithful students of Spanish at the Moline YMCA. He always came to class early and stayed late, but I doubt that he ever learned to say, "Buenos dias." I didn't even get a good opportunity to say "gracias" for all of his efforts in my behalf.

When he found out that I could not get my citizenship papers because of our illegal immigration, he went into a frenzy of activity in my behalf. He wrote hundreds of letters. He visited all of the Illinois congressmen, senators, as well as all of the state legislators from Rock Island County. He wrote to all of the superintendents of schools of the towns where we had lived in Texas, Montana, and Iowa. He wrote to the Department of Naturalization and Immigration Service in Washington, DC.

Nearly always the advice was to the effect that I should return to Mexico, and try to come back legally into the United States. Of course there was always the cautionary addendum that I might never be permitted legal entry because of our illegal entry in the first place. So, we decided that I should "sit tight."

Finally, in 1940, Lyndon Johnson (a U.S. congressman at the time) authored a Congressional bill that became a law, and gave me a chance for American citizenship without risking going back to Mexico.

The law simply provided that any person who had documentary evidence of good citizenship and continuous residence in the U.S. since 1920 might apply for a Certificate of Legal Residence. This certificate would then qualify that person to apply for the first of three citizenship documents, and the final one would give him American citizenship.

With Carroll's help, I applied immediately, and all of the letters which he had written showed an uninterrupted record of school attendance by me since 1920. That cleared the most difficult hurdle on my road to citizenship. Of course, I had to wait for three years before the final papers were issued to me. By that time, I was in the U.S. Army Air Forces in Oklahoma City.

I doubt whether Carroll Hicks ever knew how his untiring efforts succeeded. When I finally returned to Moline after the War, I looked up his telephone number and dialed it with the following result.

"Hello. Is this Carroll Hicks' residence?"

"Yes."

"May I speak to him?"

"You may not!"

I was stunned speechless and hung up the receiver. I tried again using a slightly different approach, but the results were the same. On several other occasions I tried to introduce myself first and state the nature of my call, but I never succeeded in conveying my heartfelt appreciation to Carroll Hicks. His last favor was typical of the generous man I knew. He provided all of the flowers for my wedding, free of charge.

Gets First Citizenship Papers After Long Fight to Establish Legal Entry

—Times Photo

Jack Cervantes shown looking at his first citizenship papers which he just received.

A long fight to obtain U. S. citizenship has been brought to a successful conclusion by Jack Cervantes, 27-year-old Moline man and a native of Mexico, who has just received his first naturalization papers.

Scores of people became interested in the popular young Moline man's behalf, and approximately 2,000 letters have been written in the last four years in the attempt to prove his long-established residence and his legal entry into the United States.

One of the chief difficulties in his fight to win citizenship was the lack of a passport showing he had entered the country legally. According to members of his family, Cervantes came into the United States in 1920 when he was five years old, settling in Texas. Later the family resided in Montana and Spirit Lake, Ia., before moving to Moline in 1925.

University Graduate

Young Cervantes was graduated at the Moline high school, attended Augustana college for two years, and received his bachelor's and master's degrees at the University of Illinois in 1938 and 1939.

Cervantes encountered his first snag with his alien status in 1934 when he attempted to enlist in the air corps but was barred because of his non-citizenship. La-ter at the University of Illinois the trouble led school authorities to assess him alien tuition fees, which are double the amount paid by Illinois residents. He was also prevented from obtaining NYA aid and lack of citizenship stood in the way of obtaining positions as a high school teacher of Spanish and French, which he speaks fluently.

Aided by Many

Returning to Moline three years ago his case interested prominent quad-city people including Carroll Hicks of Carbon Cliff, N. L. MacDonald, secretary of the Moline Y. M. C. A., Judge L. E. Telleen, Miss M. Josephine Holland, principal of the Ericsson and Irving schools, W. J. Coultas, and others.

Despite this concerted effort results were slow in forthcoming and at one time it was suggested that Cervantes might have to return to Mexico and make a new entry into the United States under the regular immigration quota.

Subsequent investigations, however, substantiated Cervantes' claim to have resided in the United States since 1920 and immigration officers recently agreed to naturalization proceedings after issuing a certificate of legal entry, which gives aliens rights which usually go with a passport.

Davenport Daily Times, June 20, 1942

~ ~ ~

I was the oldest and the third in our family to go into military service. Leonard went first. He tried to enlist in the Coast Guard, but was rejected for color blindness. When that occurred, I recalled that I had met his art teacher in the locker room at the YMCA, and feeling positive about getting a good report, I asked Mr. James how Leonard was doing in his class. His reply caused me considerable chagrin and bewilderment.

"He really won't follow instructions."

"Really?" I asked dumbfounded.

"Really," the teacher replied. "I tell him to do something with his colors, and he invariably does the opposite of what I suggest."

I never knew Leonard to be insubordinate or disobedient in any way. I did remember that we were wallpapering our front room once when we ran out of paper. We sent Leonard to the store to buy a couple more rolls. When he returned with the paper, the pattern was the same, but the colors were different. Since then, I've often wondered why art teachers don't give their students color charts to discover whether any of them may be color blind.

On the other hand, as a language teacher, I never gave my students any hearing tests, although it was always evident to me that musically inclined students picked up the nuances of the spoken language much sooner than those without "an ear for music." Maybe it's more fun to try to teach the unteachable. I'm always amazed at how many schools have opted to give up intelligence testing. Even when they do give such tests they quickly become defensive and attempt to denigrate and minimize their importance.

Leonard went into the 30th (XXX) Infantry Division of the U.S. Army in 1942. Mike was assigned to the field artillery.

I was even then somewhat of a pacifist, and I halfway sympathized with Charles Lindbergh's leadership of the America First Committee. I remembered how proud all Moliners had been of his heroic flight across the Atlantic in 1927. Moline honored the "Lone Eagle" with a parade which went right down 5th Avenue. I remembered seeing him waving from an open-topped Packard convertible limousine which I believe belonged to H.C. Good. I sympathized with him, too, because of the kidnapping of his infant son. In his pictures he always seemed imperturbable but lonely, and I was sorry to see so many who had once worshiped him as a hero, now turn on him as a traitor.

All Moliners that I knew were patriotic, but there was no jingoism among them. Their patriotism was strong and silent. There was an automatic acceptance of the draft and the expectation that each would do his duty and give up his life if need be. Of course, many volunteered both as individuals and in specialized groups.

As a college graduate, I had been offered commissions in the Army and in the Navy before both of my brothers went into the service, but I was still suffering from my hernia and my alien status, so I doubt that I would have been accepted. Later, when the John Deere Battalion was formed, I could have joined that group, but I somehow got the idea that it would be repairing tractors or doing some mechanical tasks.

As a youth, I had become a Civil War buff from reading books on the subject from the Moline Public Library. I reveled in the heroics of "Stonewall" Jackson and in the gallantry of Pickett's charge. It didn't matter to me that they were Southerners. So was Albert Johnston, Longstreet, Ewell, Hill, and Stuart. Actually, I admired them more than I admired McClelland, Burnside, Sherman, or Grant. The Union soldiers had all of the advantages of superiority in numbers, supplies, transportation, territory, stability of government, and allies. The Southerners fought mostly on grit and guts. Their bravado was so exciting to me that I dreamed of becoming such a soldier in a similar war. I developed a compelling desire to share in such a struggle. The horrors of war were less intimidating to me than the fear that I would never have the chance to participate in battle.

January of 1943 saw most Moliners in the icy grip of World War II. No longer did even the most rosy-colored optimists believe that the war would be won either cheaply or quickly. Right after Pearl Harbor, our senior bookkeeper, an older man by the name of Johnson, had predicted that America would utterly route Japan in three weeks' time. Slowly and inexorably almost everyone was involved in the war effort.

Deere & Company's Export Department slowed down to a walk. Nearly all of Moline's factories turned to producing war related materials. All of them were suddenly looking for help. Men and women frequently worked one shift in one factory, and a different shift in another one. I started working a second job as a time and material expediter for the Herman Nelson Corporation, which was busily putting out space heaters to be sent to Alaska and other cold weather Allied bases.

As more and more young men left for the service, I knew that I must go, too. Tom had been rejected because of his weakened heart. I went to Dr. Costigan for a herniotomy which put me in the hospital for 15 days.

The day I was released I appeared before my draft board to tell them that my hernia was now repaired. It didn't take long for them to reexamine me and find me fit for service. I was married the day before my induction at Camp Grant, Illinois. And that was the end of my legal residence in Moline.

Wedding Day: May 27, 1943

Author with his bride, Mildred Gneier

**In New Guinea with the Fifth Air Force, in front of captured
Japanese Zero fighter plane**

Left to right: Hughes, Rosen, Author, Muhleisen

Four sons go to war. All return!

Left to right, standing: Tom, Mike, Daniel; seated: Author, Mother,
Leonard

Chapter 9

Patriotism

As my mailing address changed from Camp Grant, Illinois, to Amarillo Field, Texas, to Sioux Falls Air Base, South Dakota, to Will Rogers Field, Oklahoma, to Camp Stoneman near Pittsburg, California, to Lae, New Guinea, to Tacloban on Leyte, to Manila on Luzon, to Okinawa and Ie Shima on the Japanese Ryukyu Islands, my heart remained in Moline.

I wrote frequently to my brothers, sisters, and friends, as well as to my dear teachers, Miss Josephine Holland and Miss Marjorie Hendee. The dreams and hopes of returning to fulfill my own ambition and the expectation of my sponsors never quite left me.

I had so wrapped myself in this Horatio Alger blanket that I longed to return heroically to give credit for my success to all my benefactors in Moline. I practically forgot about my last great speech on the occasion of Mexico's Independence Day celebration, September 16, 1942. I had been asked to be the principal speaker at an occasion that was really only an excuse for another Mexican Dance.

When I arrived at the hall and watched the bedlam of kids of all ages running helter-skelter throughout the hall, older persons knotted in small groups avidly discussing the latest war news and gossip, and the younger folks trying to be both coy and noticeable to members of the opposite sex, I knew my speech would be un-welcome and unwanted. Furthermore, there was no system of amplification, and I barely heard myself introduced over the ca-cophony of sounds that reverberated from one end of the hall to the other. There was no escape. I took center stage, put my hands on my hips, and screamed out the following sentiments in Span-ish:

"I'm glad to be here, because there's so much happiness here! We're celebrating the first day of Mexico's independence because we love freedom, and that's why most of us left Mexico! It was for freedom such as we enjoy here that Father Hidalgo started the Mexican Revolution in 1810. Unhappily, he didn't see any of his dreams realized because he was executed in 1811. So, sacrifice and hard work don't always pay off, but I think that Father Hidalgo would be ashamed of those here who make no effort to improve themselves.

"The self-defeatists among us find comfort in blaming racism, and in turning their patriotic fervor once a year toward a nation we have actually abandoned. That's a lot easier than working hard to build a better image of ourselves in this country which most of us have chosen to adopt. I know that such malcontents are few, but their voices are stridently loud. Sometimes, we even tend to forget that within this assembly hall we can point to many in-dividuals who are models of success and excellence in their own fields of endeavor.

"Outside of this hall, there is also ample evidence of success among our people everywhere. This is true in most jobs and pro-fessions including Hollywood stardom. I'm sure you have all watched Dolores Del Río, Lupe Vélez, Ramon Novarro, Antonio Moreno, Ricardo Cortez, and many other Mexican movie stars who are envied by the public at large.

"The truth is that a person's success whether here in Moline or elsewhere is gained through his own efforts. Today, we rightfully celebrate the original call for Mexico's independence, but we all know deep in our hearts that in the United States we have found real freedom every day!"

There was no show of understanding or emotion. Actually, the crowd had politely quieted while I spoke. The sporadic clapping was just an acknowledgment of the end of my speech and a hope that the dance would begin soon. As I descended the steps from the stage, Ynez Bargas clasped my hand and with trembling voice implored, "Please, don't bother to speak to these burros again!" I never did.

However, I did feel compelled to give one more bit of advice. One of my brother Daniel's friends, wrote me the following handwritten letter. I haven't corrected several grammatical errors, and the ten erasures and mark-overs will not show:

Dear Mr. Cervantes:

Please do not think me to forward in writing you, but Dan said that you would be willing to help me. Perhaps if I told you a little about myself you will be able to advise me better. I received my B.E. from a teachers college June 1949, where I majored in social science and minored in Spanish. I was unable to find employment because it seems that school boards aren't very eager to hire Mexicans. Recently I have taken a civil service exam, however employment depends upon my acceptance into a graduate school. It has been suggested that I go out of the state. This is where I would like your help. Would I be accepted at U.C.L.A. with a C. average? Are there other advantages in Calif.? That is other than going to school and teaching for a Mexican. I'm very determined to do something with the education I have, however there doesn't seem to be the opportunity here. Thank you for listening you have been very kind and I will sincerely appreciate any advise, however please don't think I am sorry I am a Mexican, perhaps it is only bitterness

Sincerely yours,
(Miss) XXXX XXXXXXXXXX

I promptly replied as follows:

Dear Miss XXXXXXXXX:

This will acknowledge your letter which I find exceedingly difficult to answer because I don't know you, and I am, therefore, inferring much that may be untrue. I assume that you have been unsuccessful in finding a teaching position in the State of Illinois.

I agree with you that the school boards, "Aren't very eager to hire Mexicans." Why should they be, when their job is to hire teachers? Remember that they have a duty to provide for the taxpayers, the parents, and the children of their school district the very best in instructional personnel that they can afford. Wherever your application failed, more than likely somebody else's succeeded. Can you honestly rule out the possibility that the successful applicants may have had better preparation and more to offer these communities than you did?

Your "C" grade average to most people means that your scholarly attainments were only mediocre, and most graduate schools would think twice before accepting you as a candidate for an advanced degree.

Here I must again infer that you have prepared to teach at the secondary level. If my guess is correct, your choice of subject matter and grade level have been quite unfortunate. Enclosed, herein, I am sending you a clipping from today's "Los Angeles Times", substantiating the fact that even well-prepared teachers of the Mayflower stock are going jobless in your subject field at the secondary level. Actually, most tenured secondary school teachers in California hold a Masters Degree or its equivalent.

Now about the question of prejudice, I can only cite the following facts. I only knew four other Mexicans who were graduated with me from the School of Education at the University of Illinois. All of us are teaching. I am the only one working outside of Illinois. I'll be glad to give you the names and addresses of the others in case you should want to communicate with them.

You also ask me, "Whether there are any other advantages in California?" If you mean for Mexicans, probably not. If you mean for teachers, absolutely yes! The recent influx of people into this State continues to be remarkable. The birth rate is also quite high. Therefore, it has been necessary to build and staff schools in record numbers. Most people who come here like the climate, and even teachers' salaries are showing slight improvement.

However, if you expect your heritage to compensate for any personal inadequacies you may feel, you'll probably find life more unbearable here than you have ever known it to be in Illinois. California's history is rife with examples of racial intolerance; toward Chinese, Japanese, East Indians, and especially toward Mexicans. As a matter of fact, the recent surges of anti-Mex-ican feeling have been more pronounced here and in Texas than elsewhere in the whole United States. So, here's the best advice I can give you.

1. If you really want to teach, get rid of your inferiority complex and concentrate on becoming a superior teacher. Remember that when you need an operation you want the best surgeon available, regardless of his ethnicity. Similarly, boards of education are always looking for the best teach-ers they can get.

2. Survey the teaching field, and prepare to teach in those areas where teachers are most in demand. Currently more teachers are needed in the elementary level or in the home economics or the vocational areas of the secondary schools cur-ricula. Even if you have to retrace some of your educational steps, it's always more advantageous to be in demand than to be demanding.

3. Boost your grade average, because that is practically the sole criterion of an inexperi-enced teacher's worth.

4. Join several teachers employment agencies. The commission you pay them for your first job may hold the key to your future success.

5. Keep in touch with me, particularly if you expect to come here.

6. Strengthen your faith in yourself, in your abilities, and in your resolution to succeed. With God's help you cannot fail.

I never received a reply. Much later, I showed my son Charles this exchange of communications, because he works as a public defender among Mexicans and other minorities with low images of personal worth. I rather got the impression from him that all of the answers I gave her were wrong. They probably were. Yet, I could only answer from the depths of my personal convictions. These ideas were formed, nurtured, and established before I left Moline.

Perhaps I should have encouraged her to hurry out to California. She might have become the chairman of the Chicano Studies program at UCLA. My youngest son Paul, who is currently trying to become the fifth of my children to graduate from UCLA, claims that there are certain advantages there if you're willing to claim being disadvantaged by your ethnicity. My son John Jr. laughingly proclaims that Fresno State, where he is currently enrolled, has a department of Armenian Studies. Truly the squeaky wheel seems to be getting most of the grease. Was this always so — everywhere?

As a professional teacher and member of the first Human Relations Council of the Los Angeles City Schools, I've always fought for the kind of equality that didn't require an ethnic handicap to be even. I must also admit that my position was always overruled by the self-styled liberals who have wanted to force others to do their will. Others should integrate their schools and communities, others should give up their own jobs and promotions, others should forego their opportunities for training in skilled and professional schools.

I never could get anyone to share my convictions that most self-styled liberals are the biggest bigots of all! They hold a surreptitiously cavalier attitude of condescension toward whole groups of people who may be of minority background, poor, aged, etc. This attitude is expressed by their transparent feeling of sympathy and concern for all members of that underprivileged group. Actually, it appears to be an attempt to elevate their own sense of worth and importance. It seems that they want to climb a social ladder so they can be looked up at while they look down benignly upon a whole group of inferior beings.

Of course every such minority has individuals who will cater to these liberals for profit or selfish interest. My cousin Hilda Hilario tells a story about her second son, Raymond, that illustrates this point comically.

As a grade school student, Raymond noticed that all of the Mexican children in his class received free milk through some federal program for migrant students. One day he came home from school and complained bitterly to his mother about his sister Patricia.

"Mother, Patsy must have told the teacher on me."

"Told her what, Raymond?"

"That I was a Mexican."

"Well, how do you know that?"

"Because, today they gave me the milk."

Raymond grew up and became a reasonably well-educated man with the kind of complexion and accent that would permit him to pass as any kind of "Anglo" that he would like to be. He married an "Anglo" girl, and he became a teacher. When I met him after the latest political Chicano chicanery, Raymond had been divorced from his first wife, married a girl named Rosa, found a job as a school principal, earned a Ph. D., and went by the name of Ramon. *O tempora, o mores!*

When I was appointed to the Council of Human Relations for the Los Angeles City Schools, I really believed that I would have the opportunity to present some simple truths that I always used to guide my actions. The most basic tenet of my beliefs is that some members of any designated group are well-adjusted, successful, happy, and respected as individuals. Such persons need neither special sympathy nor special programs from anyone.

There are always other individuals in any group whose handicaps are so severe that no amount of sympathy or special help will ever equalize their opportunities to excel even among those who are regarded as being average.

Those that remain between these two extremes must each find his own individual destiny in his own individual way. Any attempt to categorize them, to lump them together, to provide them with the same help, solely on one given characteristic such as ethnicity will surely fail. Furthermore, many in all minority groups find such stereotypical images both demeaning and demoralizing.

Whenever I have articulated my dismay at all of this ethnic over-concern by government, by industry, by schools, and by well-meaning individuals, I am always amazed at the obvious implications of their replies. They mask the reverse discriminatory practices of affirmative action programs, but what I really understand is that:

1. Government wants to play up to the minorities in order to get their votes.
2. The schools want minorities' program money from the government.
3. Industry wants the minorities' money.
4. Personally inadequate people need minorities as their scapegoat.
5. Minority persons who may have felt discrimination want revenge.
6. Some members of ethnic minorities want all the leverage they can get in order to advance their own selfish concerns.

Life in the Moline that I knew had none of this sophistry.

Short and long of the P.U.G. Fraternity, 1936

Find Author and Harry Mead

CHAPTER 10

RETURN

You can never go back to Moline. I've returned regularly for 41 years, but I find that my Moline was either the figment of my imagination or the creature of my dreams. Each time I returned to see Mother and my brothers and sisters, I discovered changes that were disquieting.

The most obvious changes were the slow, steady decay of what I remember as downtown. Whereas, when we first arrived, there were passenger trains bringing people to Moline and transporting them from Moline several times a day from the waiting rooms of three different railroad lines, now there are no passenger trains serving this area. Actually, only the Milwaukee station remains, and this houses an office for Franks Foundries.

Whereas, there used to be regular streetcar service from the easternmost part of Moline to its westernmost boundary and all the way south to the end of 15th Street, not even the streetcar tracks remain.

Whereas, 5th Avenue was always full of shoppers and gawkers from daylight to dark, now there are only a few people gathered around struggling stores that once used to be among the proud enterprises of the Quad Cities. The New York Store, Fisk & Loosely, F.W. Woolworth, and Carson Pirie Scott & Co. are now all gone.

The names of Josephson Jewelers, Ranks Shoe Store, Schwenker & Mougin, and Fitzgibbon's Men's Wear still appear over the storefronts, but these just resemble doddering old dowagers valiantly attempting to keep up a recognizable front. Even the two banks on the corner of 5th Avenue and 15th Street look like they're ready for demolition. At least one-fourth of all the downtown business concerns I knew have already been demolished and turned into parking lots.

The library still presents a formidable and healthy appearance, and the *Moline Daily Dispatch* building actually looks better than ever. All of the theaters in downtown Moline are gone. The YMCA is gone. The LeClaire Hotel is closed. Central Grammar has been demolished, the Allendale mansion houses the administrative offices of the Moline Public Schools, and the Moline High School building has irrevocably been depraved into an office complex and is now known as the Beling Building.

All of my brothers deserted Moline. Daniel moved to California, Leonard went to Bettendorf, and Michael lives in Davenport. Only my sisters Margaret and Mary remain in Moline. My half-sister Ramona moved to Antioch, Illinois.

What creeping malady is slowly strangling my Moline? While the whole nation has more than doubled in population, Moline has barely gained one-fourth more in population than it had in 1939. My brother Michael, who is currently the housing inspection supervisor for the City of Davenport, feels that the main reason for Moline's atrophy has been its failure to diversify its industry.

The agricultural implement business continues to be the bread and butter of Moline's working population, but the area is beset by slowdowns, shutdowns, and layoffs. Whenever the farmer falters, Moline hurts!

Evidently other factors also contributed to the paucity of opportunities. Obviously, Moline has been landlocked by its natural and man-made boundaries, but where is the renewal? Only the ribbons of I-74 and the parking lots scattered all over town seem to have regular life and vitality.

My end of Moline is now a depressed area. Where all the proud west-enders refused to go on relief through the darkest days of the Great Depression, we now find all kinds of recipients of federal and county largesse.

Mother doesn't live at 518 Railroad Avenue anymore, even though she still pays for all of the utilities in that empty house where she says she has, "all of her things." Over 90 percent of the people in that neighborhood are recent Mexican immigrants, thus making it a "barrio" in the American newspaper sense of the word. This barrio now extends from 1st Street to 10th Street on all avenues north of 5th Avenue. I know Mother will never return to live there. She doesn't like the area. She doesn't know any of these new foreigners, and has no desire to become acquainted with them.

Even Ericsson School has been taken over by the new Latinos. Such has been the infiltration of do-gooder programs that government-paid personnel have come to Mother's door to tell her of her rights and how to demand them. She can even go to St. Mary's to hear a Mass in Spanish — after all the time Mrs. Anan spent teaching her English — so she could become a citizen of the United States, and vote an English-written ballot. Too bad we got here so soon. Now we could go to Ericsson and learn bilingual nonsense syllables.

Most of all, I see Moline society fragmentized in a way I never knew it to be before. Even my brother-in-law Richard Peterson found his sons work on the railroad under an affirmative action program where ethnic preference was the order of the day. I guess

Richard Jr. got the job as a minority person even though he became Vi-King at Augie the year he was a senior. Of course Augie was in on the lark too, because they chose a "negro" student for that honor several years later.

Maybe my Moline is trying to keep up with the rest of the country that had two black Miss Americas in 1984 and a black Queen of the Tournament of Roses Parade in Pasadena, California. This young lady was interviewed on television shortly after her selection and asked how she felt about being the first black Rose Bowl Queen. She replied to the effect that she much preferred to be just the Rose Bowl Queen.

Mother and I long for my Moline of equal opportunity for all, including the so-called whites or "Anglos." We remember the beauty of living on 5th Street and Railroad Avenue where each of our neighbors was of a different nationality, and each family spoke a different language among themselves and within their national groups, but both children and adults used every opportunity to learn the language of their adopted country. Today, before a bank in East Moline I saw four flags of equal size on equal masts all flying at the same height. These were the flags of the United States of America, Sweden, Belgium, and Mexico. My Moline has changed!

Most of my college-graduated nieces and nephews have left Moline. Rick Peterson and Jesse Lopez have gone to Chicago. Paul Peterson went to Dallas, Texas. Leonard practices law in St. Louis, while his brother Edward works in Cedar Rapids. Michael and Pamela teach in Davenport, but their brother Daniel takes the prize. He recruits the best talent available for Texas Instruments and takes them off to Dallas, Texas. My own children, as well as my brother Daniel's children are irretrievably ensconced in California. Mother has about 35 college-educated grandchildren, but most of them have moved away from Moline.

Maybe it's just as well. Some historians claim that Spain did not lose its status as a world power because of England's triumph over the Spanish Armada, but rather because so many of its young men left to establish colonies in the New World. Maybe Mother's progeny is also establishing new colonies. If so, I know that they will carry the spirit of Moline wherever they go, because the spirit of Moline lives on!

John Deere's spirit certainly thrives in its new administrative center on John Deere Road. Among its awards for excellence of design, it won First Honor award from the American Institute of Architects in 1965. Two years before its vice president Bud Lundahl died, I had lunch with him in the magnificent cafeteria overlooking its man-made lake complete with ducks. The following year, he took me on another tour of the additional wing which had just been completed. I always used to cringe when I brought foreign customers to the old Export Department on 3rd Avenue. How proudly they display this new magnificent complex to tourists and buyers from all over the world who come to visit today.

The Quad Cities Airport is another success story that Moline can proudly claim. I watched the rivalry between Cram Field and the Moline Airport for many years, but now I have arrived and departed from the Quad Cities Airport, and I know that this airport will continue to be one of the Midwest's important stations.

Buses have replaced streetcars for the indigent traveler of short distances, while automobiles and airplanes have replaced the passenger trains for the traveler of longer distances. In Moline, as in most other civilized cities of the world, the automobile has also virtually replaced the pedestrian.

My Moline was a pedestrian city. People walked up and down

all of the city streets, and crowds walked up and down 5th Avenue and 15th Street. The great avenues of transportation, the River and the railroads, were close to the great avenues of commerce. The better residential homes were away from the busy bustle of both commerce and transportation, while the more modest homes were located adjacent and among the places where their owners worked. But the sidewalks were used by all!

Recently, I've walked the length of 4th and 5th Avenues where the old streetcars ran. The broad ribbons of concrete for the automobile are constantly being repaired and upgraded, while the narrow sidewalks for the pedestrians have virtually been abandoned. On 4th Avenue, from 55th Street to 23rd Street, the sidewalks are not continuous on either side of the street. These were either never built or they have disappeared. On the other side of 4th Avenue between 38th and 26th Streets, grass grows abundantly between the cracks so that these sidewalks have been reduced to stepping stones. On 26th Street, I saw a homeowner busily mowing his sidewalks!

The bridge abutments and the supporting columns of I-74 have further denigrated my Moline. The broad, smooth white lanes of concrete dedicated to the automobile have left black, ugly monstrous spaces beneath. These caverns are more fit for the denizens of hell than for the pedestrians of my Moline. If left that way, I can foresee bats flying around its dark recesses while rats burrow below. The only ones apparently interested in these cement walls are the graffiti artists.

These and other highways may yet be the salvation of my Moline. Like any aging body, she may have needed a heart transplant. I witnessed its old, narrow arterial streets become increasingly clogged with foot and auto traffic. Now, the stench of auto exhaust has for the most part moved to South Park and the other shopping areas along 23rd Avenue. Shakespeare was right:

"Money is always welcome, even when it stinks."

More than likely it was monied interests that built my Moline in the first place. Will these interests also destroy her? Why did Moline High School, the YMCA, and Black Hawk College choose to establish their new homes in the most remote corner of Moline? Were they all imbued with the desire to leave the old behind as far as possible in search of the new? How much was dictated by the profit motive?

Age can also have dignity, grace, and beauty. I'm always inspired by my return trips to old St. Mary's Church. Here I never feel old! In deep meditation, people here see themselves in the mirror of their minds, and to themselves their personalities and their appearances never change, even when their former friends and neighbors fail to recognize them.

At Mass I am always the child of the Lord! The priest is the right hand of God as he raises the host and the wine to consecrate them into the body and blood of Jesus Christ. Here I am reinvigorated and rededicated to the religion of my youth and of my ancestors. Here, I fervently pray that my own children will find the same comfort, the same solace, and the same meaning of life that became my guiding light.

Here I weep bitterly and silently for those of my children who apparently look upon my faith as some kind of modern mythology. My most precious beliefs have been frustrated and betrayed! I helplessly see them observing the Sabbath, Thanksgiving Day, Christmas, Easter, and other religious Holy Days as convenient vacations from their usual pursuits. I hope against hope that I am mistaken, and that a tiny spark within them will someday renew that faith which their mother and I tried to instill into their youthful spirits.

Outside of the church I become old once more. The glaring mundane daylight surrounds me, and even the priest loses his mantle of holiness and becomes an ordinary fallible man. When he tells me that Masses in Spanish are essential because there are many parishioners who have lived here for 50 and 60 years who do not speak English, I feel like turning professorial and asking him to, "Name three." I choose not to embarrass him. I know all of the Spanish speaking people who still remain in the parish since 1925. He doesn't!

Instead, I go to Mother's house with her, my wife Mildred, my sisters Mary and Margaret, and my brother-in-law Dick Peterson. We are looking for old mementos and pictures to amplify this writing. We find my old Class A Caddie pin, #41. Its silver finish has not tarnished. I note that it was made in New York. We find three cardboard-framed pictures of classmates I considered to be my best high school friends — Jack Railsback, his cousin Tad Railsback, and Dick Beitel, our senior class president. I hope to take these and other memorabilia to our 50-year class reunion.

Author's Class A Caddie pin, #41

I also find two of my old neighbors still living next-door to Mother's vacant house. They are George and Theda Tertipes. We reminisce about our families and about our old neighbors. It's all pleasantly light-hearted, sincere warm exchange of news and banter. Finally, its time for me to leave and I have found that most of the Tertipes family has also left Moline. We all embrace briefly and self-consciously echoing hopes of meeting again.

George notes that, "The neighborhood has really changed."

Theda adds, "We used to be such good neighbors. Now, others around here look upon us suspiciously and call us 'the white people.' Imagine, we're now called 'the white people.'"

I thought I detected a sad note of irony at their being promoted from our Greek neighbors to "the white people."

The greatest single change I note is that the person-oriented society that I knew as a young man has now become increasingly impersonal. When we first arrived in Moline we immediately made many personal acquaintances with individuals in the community who seemed to be glad to help us get established. We moved four times before I was graduated from Moline High School, and each time we left the old neighborhood, we continued the friendships with those who had helped us.

A case in point: one of our first grocers, Jennie Taets, not only continued to be interested in our family long after her husband died and she left their grocery store, but almost 60 years after we first met, she has written to me from Tennessee to express interest in this writing and to contribute a picture of their first store in Moline.

The next change I notice is that currently, if a person needs help he is generally referred to a government agency or to some special interest group. It appears that the day when one individual helped another one out of his own resources has largely become a thing of the past. In this respect, I don't imagine that Moline is much different from most towns and cities in the United States.

I have written about the small area of Moline that I knew best as a boy, but I realize that there are other areas which I never knew well before, and that these areas seem to hold considerable promise of enhancing the quality of life for many different classes of Moliners. Recreational activities seem to be more widely used. This is especially obvious at the park and boat launching area next to the Mississippi River. The bike-jog trail that runs from 7th Street near the Rock River and back north on 60th Street to John Deere Road also shows promise. This area of Moline is where the greatest growth in new construction is taking place. The largest shopping mall is in South Park, and nice homes have already been built in Wildwood, Homewood, and other similar sub-divisions.

Moline still needs a golf course, better tourist accommodations, and live entertainment facilities such as theaters, but it seems that Moliners who want such things can and do go to Rock Island, Davenport, Chicago, Las Vegas, or Hawaii.

Its educational complexes are evidently holding out hope to both young and old. A Black Hawk College bulletin shows the picture of 70-year-old Wladystaw Schab who walks from Silvis to the Moline Adult Learning Center even when the temperature is below zero. Evidently, Moline is still helping people who help themselves. Maybe it's just as well that she cannot take care of all her chicks. Like a mother bird, she sees it best to push them out of her warm nest to go forth and serve other people in other places.

When one sees the same faces in the same places, day in and day out, year after year, change is so gradual as to seem almost imperceptible. My 62-year-old brother Leonard can't read a menu in a reasonably well-lit restaurant, but he proudly proclaims that he doesn't need glasses yet. We attended a recent reunion of caddies at the Rock Island Arsenal Golf Club where he caddied only one year and I caddied six years. Without glasses he recognized all of his caddy friends, but even with glasses, I couldn't recognize any of the men I had associated with as a boy for so long a period of time. I wouldn't even have recognized Gus Flider, except that Leonard pointed him out to me. Then I saw that he still stood straight, tall, slender, and smiling. He had changed least of all in outward appearance, and not at all in charm and personality. He even went out of his way to get me a copy of a booklet about the Rock Island Arsenal Golf Club which was first printed in 1906.

It was at this reunion that I also found out that there had been no caddies employed there for more than 35 years. No wonder young boys are finding it tough to find employment, but more importantly, the youth of today have that many fewer opportunities to meet the really successful people of their community as ordinary people in need of relaxing recreation.

I had previously attended a reunion of war buddies. We have been meeting annually over the past few years. There was no trouble in recognition among any of us. We have become more or less members of the same family because we've met at each others' homes and have remained in touch via letters, pictures, phone calls, and visits with each other.

Such was not the case at my 50-year Moline High School class reunion. In spite of having attended these reunions faithfully every five years since 1949, I couldn't recognize the majority of my classmates. A few had not changed a great deal in appearance. I think all of us recognized Frank Byers, Dick Beitel, Bill Bimson, Oscar DeCloedt, and Bill Hart on sight. The girls' appearance seemed to have changed more, but of course I did recognize a few of them too. Margaret Castle really hasn't changed much, in spite of or because of her marriage to Swede Aim. If it's true that people of opposite personalities are attracted to each other, then they were a perfect match. I also recognized a girl I don't remember seeing since we were in the same 5th grade class. Her name is Mary Lou Howlett, and later I found out that this was the first reunion she had ever attended. It was also the first reunion attended by Dave Dobson, Vernon Remlin, and several others.

In spirit and in personality, I doubt that any of us changed at all. The big wheels of the class were still turning things on. In numbers they had been most effective in producing a great turnout. The shy, bashful ones were still reclusive. Jane Wallace said to me, "Remember me? I was the quiet one, but I'm not quiet any more!" However, I didn't hear or see any more of her, even though I should have loved to chat with her.

I had met Betty Kirk at the Rock Island County Historical Society, and had told her I'd see her at the reunion, but I never did. I wanted to thank Rosemary Ward for her help in several situations where I needed help prior to the reunion, but I didn't get a chance to do that either. Later, she sent me a clipping from the *Moline Daily Dispatch* about my attempts to publish this book.

I think we found out that night what all people eventually discover. At all stages of our lives, we have too little time! Among my classmates we could have pointed out examples of great success stories. In every part of that congregation there were some of the best of lawyers, doctors, dentists, nurses, engineers, geologists, etc. No one mentioned these accomplishments. Each one of us hungered only for the retelling of little old stories that wouldn't die, because they had formed our character and the substance of our generation.

On September 15, 1984, we had a chance to tour the building where we went to high school. I was impressed with this massive, solid, brick structure and the thick noiseless cement construction of its floors, walls, and ceilings. This ample, solid, sturdy and soundproof feeling was especially noticeable in the auditorium, the gymnasium, the stairs, and the broad hallways.

The views of the area of Moline which used to inspire me as I gazed from the north windows were still lovely to my eyes. I was amazed to learn that the building had been sold for less than $50,000. I'm sure they couldn't rebuild just the gym for twice that sum today. The auditorium, the chemistry lab, and the gym appeared largely unchanged. When we looked down onto the gym floor from its surrounding elevated track, I knew that I couldn't resist taking one last lap. Frank Byers must have had the same idea, because we started to run it simultaneously. For a few moments we shook away 50 years and recaptured the joy of our youth.

At the dinner, Oscar DeCloedt was the center of attention among the athletes. He had kept some issues of the Moline High School newspaper, the *Line O' Type*, from 1934. In it were events that would yank most of our memories back 50 years. Oscar yelled out to Dave Dobson, "Remember the football game we played against LaSalle?"

"Yeah, Bill Hart wrecked his knee."

"I guess they wrecked most of us. Look at that score: Moline 7, Lasalle 38."

Next, Oscar turns to another issue of the *Line O' Type*, shows it to me, and asks, "Do you remember anyone here?"

I answer, "Well, I'll be darned! Here, let me borrow it for a minute. I'll bring it right back."

"Don't lose it," he cautions. "Bring it back to me. I'll be right here."

The room was crammed with little knots of people speaking hurriedly and avidly. Each person wanting to share moments from the past with those in front, yet looking around for others to speak to next. I spot Anna Mae Hemmingson and Shirley Frank. They're in different groups talking animatedly.

Chills, Thrills, Romance, Laughter in "Tiger House"

DRAMATIC CLUB TO GIVE PLAY FRIDAY, MAY 4

Play Will Be Given May 4

Creepy Noises, Eerie Lights, Clutching Claws Atmosphere To Sensational Drama

"Creepy noises, eerie lights, women's screams and clutching claws that snatch unsuspecting characters off the stage right before your very eyes," are only a few of the thrills you will experience when you see that famous mystery comedy play, "Tiger House," to be presented Friday, May 4, by the Dramatic Club in the high school auditorium.

But don't be afraid! Of course, you will be excited. You might even scream! But just when you expect the worst you will start laughing at some of the rib-tickling comedy which always comes along

The cast of the hair-raising mystery, "Tiger House," to be presented as the annual production of the Dramatic Club.

Left to right (standing): Jack Cervantes, Jack Railsback, Carol Getz and Lloyd England. (Seated): Amirette Baker, Virginia Carlson, Bud Lundahl, Shirley Frank, Jim Carris, and Anna Mae Hemmingson.

The cast of *Tiger House*

Left to right, standing: Author, Jack Railsback, Carol Getz, Lloyd England; seated: Amirette Baker, Virginia Carlson, Bud Lundahl, Shirley Frank, Jim Carris, Anna Mae Hemmingson

When I show them the picture of our cast for *Tiger House*, taken in the Moline High School Auditorium, they stop talking to examine it carefully. I observe that two of the members of that cast, Jack Railsback and Bud Lundahl are now dead. I can see that this picture brings back a flood of memories to their minds as it does to mine. Some of these memories are disjointed both in time and space.

I remembered when Miss Straw took all of her 5th graders to a concert by a visiting symphony orchestra in this same auditorium back in 1927. She spent several days preparing us for this treat by showing us pictures of the different orchestral instruments. She mimicked how each would sound, and we laughed at her attempts to vocalize the sounds of the piccolo and the tympani.

When the day arrived, she noted that there were several inches of newly fallen snow. Of course, we would have to walk both ways, and we would have to be on our best behavior, especially at the concert. "Most importantly, children, you must not make snowballs, or pick up snow for any reason. If you disobey, you'll be suspended and maybe expelled. We wouldn't want anyone to be hurt for any reason, now would we?"

"No, Miss Straw," was the general reply. I shook my head and wondered just who could possibly want to disobey such reasonable expectations.

So, off we went marching in a neat double file. Everything went fine on the way to the concert and at the concert. I thoroughly enjoyed myself, especially when I recognized bits and pieces of selections my grandfather used to play on his violin.

The return trip was almost as successful, but I ruined everything as we came within sight of our building on the Grant School ground. It was such a beautiful day. The sun shone so brightly as to make our eyes blink constantly due to the glaring whiteness lying all around us. Miss Straw was striding rapidly in front of our long column. It would be just a matter of about five minutes before we would be safely in our desks having successfully complied with all of our teacher's expectations.

I felt just great. This had been such a fine day for me! Here I was in the middle of the column. I wanted most of all to express my great joy. All of the beauty of the music, the rapidly warming day, and the melting snow combined within me and cried out for some expression.

With a great surge of power, I scooped up a big handful of

snow, cupped it into a ball and hurled it over the heads of the advancing column. Naturally, I had hoped that it would land beyond the last straggler. Instead it hit Doris Knight squarely over the right eye.

She let out a long piercing cry of bewildered pain, and in the next moment both Miss Straw and I were examining the rapidly swelling and slowly discoloring eye. By the time we got into the room, it had puffed up closed and showed streaks of color ranging from yellow to purple. I expected the worst.

My mind flashed back to the only spanking I had ever received from a teacher. It occurred in a small rural Texas school as a result of a relief map we had to make on a piece of cardboard with a paste made of flour and water. We were supposed to take our water paints home to color the map after it dried, and we were supposed to get our parents to help us with this project.

When I mentioned the assignment to my parents they both jumped into the project with great and ignorant zeal. They kneaded the dough and rolled it out into a gigantic tortilla. They made mountains, lakes, and rivers just anywhere. I tried to complain and to redirect their efforts, but they were having so much fun that I just couldn't hurt their feelings. Finally, their idea of a color scheme was not to show water, mountains, and deserts, but just to make something pretty.

The next day I submitted my map with great misgivings to the teacher who examined it unbelievingly and asked, "Did your folks help you with this map?"

"Yes, Miss Jones!"

"I don't believe it. I just don't believe it! So, for lying and for poor work, you are going to be spanked."

Spanking was a daily occurrence in that school. Although this had never happened to me, I wasn't afraid. I was resentful. Waves of frustration welled up within me. I knew that I could have done this assignment very well all by myself. I had asked for my parents' help only because I wanted to do exactly as the teacher had directed. Now, I was about to be humiliated in front of the whole class, just for being obedient.

Tears rolled down my cheeks, and I'm sure that everyone in that room considered me to be a coward. Actually, I don't remember either the number of strokes or the pain inflicted by that paddling. I only remember the injustice of it all.

My mind flashed back to Moline, as I re-envisioned Miss Straw and the injured eye of Doris Knight. Surely, I deserved whatever punishment I might get, but as in the former incident, I just prayed that my parents would never know.

Strangely enough, neither Miss Straw nor Doris ever brought up that subject at all. I don't know why. I know that Miss Straw never liked Doris. Doris was an attractive little redheaded flirt, and Miss Straw always blamed her for any commotion or noise emanating from her corner of the room. Just before we were dismissed that day, Miss Straw said quietly, "Doris, tomorrow, I want you to wear your stockings up where they belong."

"I just rolled them down because it's so hot."

"I don't care how hot it is. You don't see me with my stockings rolled down around my ankles like two ugly doughnuts. Do you?"

Doris opened her mouth to protest, but Miss Straw announced that, "The class is dismissed."

I've never dismissed that incident entirely. On the one hand, I understand that I never intended to harm anyone in any way, especially Doris. On the other hand, I realize that the whole unfortunate incident was entirely my fault. She evidently forgave me as quickly as Miss Straw. Three years later, when Doris played the lead in a junior high school musical, she easily sold me tickets to her performance.

"You know, Jack, I'm going to play the lead in the play. You'll like that. Won't you?"

I did. Actually, I can still sing her two solos from *The Sunbonnet Girl*. Her opening number complained:

Washing dishes, washing dishes,
That is all I do, it seems.
Washing dishes, washing dishes,
While my head is full of dreams.

In those days, most of us experienced vague longings for unspecified, uncertain futures, full of dreams. So, we spent the whole evening of our 50-year class reunion recalling and recapturing memories that for each of us had endured for 50 and 60 years or more, but I have no idea of whatever happened to Doris Knight.

CHAPTER 11

REPRISE

The next day, my wife and I took an afternoon excursion on the Mississippi River on a paddle wheel steamboat called the *River Queen*. In two hours it traveled downstream toward Davenport and upstream to East Moline. During the entire trip we could see a veritable ocean of green trees covering my Moline.

The LeClaire Hotel still dominates that landscape. The pilot explained that we would have to navigate through a hole in "the great wall of Moline." This was one of the many early attempts to harness the waterpower of the great Mississippi River. As one looks critically at all of man's attempts to control nature, in the long run I suppose that they're all failures. Fortunately, man does not live very long. He measures his attempts in terms of hours, minutes and seconds rather than in centuries, geologic periods, or eons. This realization helps me to assuage the sorrow I feel that all of my Moline benefactors died before they could see any solid evidence of my success or failure.

My wife is not a Moliner, and so she sees Moline as any other mid-American city. I'm surprised that she still listens to all of my explanations and comparisons. Mother seems to understand, but she doesn't complain. She and Mary Josephine Holland lived by the same philosophy. They "look upon the world with quiet eyes."

I suppose that I lament the changes in Moline, because I examine too critically all that to me was once young and beautiful. It is difficult for me to accept that "beauty is in the eyes of the beholder," and that my eyes have become dim with age. Yet, what is age? My father died at 41, my stepfather died at 91, and in August of 1984, Miss Hendee wrote me the following letter:

```
Dear Jack,

    I cannot help with the book because I'm sick
and don't feel like it. I am now 94. I hope you
have success with your book. I would have loved
to do it about 3 or 4 years ago, but now it is
beyond me. I don't have the ambition. 94 is a
pretty good age and you can imagine how I feel.

    Yours Sincerely,
    Marjorie A. Hendee
```

I wonder if youth can really imagine the feelings of the aged? At what point in life does an older person quit trying? When does all hope die?

Marjorie Adele Hendee died Saturday, October 26, 1985. She was 95 years old, and had been retired from her Moline High School teaching duties since 1955. I visited her briefly at the Moline Nursing and Rehabilitation Center on Monday, October 21 and again on Tuesday, October 22.

When I first saw her sitting forlornly in a straight chair alongside her hospital bed, it struck me that she was but a shell of her former self. Her skin was sallow and hung loosely from her cheekbones, from her chin, from her arms, and even from her elbows. Her eyes were wide open, but they seemed to stare ahead without apparent interest. I greeted her, but I knew that she didn't recognize me and that she was practically stone deaf. Finally, I screamed into her ear, "I'm Jack, Jack Cervantes."

"Oh, Jack," she murmured. "Jack Cervantes, yes!" A spark of animation and recognition showed in her face. "How's the book coming?"

"It's all done," I yelled in her ear. I knew she understood, and as I watched her obvious pleasure, I turned my head so she could not see the tears of joy and sadness welling up in my own eyes. "Can you still read?" I yelled.

"Oh, yes," she answered softly, and then she added as a pleasant afterthought, "I used to be an English teacher."

When I told her that I would give her the first copy that came off the press, her face clouded over in seeming discontent. I thought that she was disappointed because I didn't have the book to give her.

"When can I go home? I want to go home," she pleaded.

"How long have you been here?"

"About a week."

"Who's taking care of you?"

"Mr. Henricksen," I thought she replied.

"Well, you'll have to ask him," I said defensively. I sat on her bed and wondered why she was tied to her chair. I tried to make small talk about her room and about the weather.

Finally, she entreated, "I want to go to bed."

"I'll tell the nurse," I replied. Then I have to go, but I'll come back to see you again tomorrow."

"Oh, that's good, and thank you!"

The next day I returned with my wife. She didn't appear to recognize me at first. When I made clear to her who I was, she asked, "And who is that?"

"It's my wife," I hollered in her ear.

"Oh," she said smiling and then tried to involve her in the conversation by asking, "How many children do you have?"

"Eight," we both replied holding up eight fingers for her to count.

"Oh," she ventured, as though embarrassed to have asked.

I tried lamely to say something pleasant and entertaining to her. Surely, I thought that there must be more than that to share after an acquaintance of better than 52 years. There wasn't! It seems that age inexorably closes one door after the other in the long hall of life's memories. As we closed the last door to the outside of that building, I half-whispered to my wife that I had just said my last goodby to Miss Hendee.

When I returned to my home in California, I received her obituary which Gus Flider had clipped for me from the *Moline Daily Dispatch*. I read and reread it several times. There was one note of joy for her and one for me. Marjorie Hendee's body had gone back to Grayslake, the land of her birth and of her youth, yet I shall always maintain with certain conviction that her spirit will continue to live in my Moline.

Yes! We're old, we're grey and wrinkled,
And sometimes quite forlorn.
To think that all the dreams we dreamed
Are often viewed with scorn.

Why, then, the struggle and the sorrow,
When our ideals seem nullified?
Perhaps, the builders of tomorrow,
Will find this truth that seems to hide.

God really is our architect,
And the maker of our laws.

He'll continue changes, I suspect
So, let's never regret the loss.

As we continued our excursion we watched the sun drift slowly toward its setting. I realized once more how much remains unchanged. Old Sol still smiles the beginning of each day for Moliners by emerging from its rolling waterbed, and it finishes its sizzling race by dipping again into its watery refuge. In its diurnal task it warms my Moline and the rest of the world. It causes the plants to bloom and the heart to sing. Only the darkest clouds have the power to obscure its face with rain or snow to provide moisture wherever it is needed. With great, unerring regularity the sun continues to move across the sky from summer solstice to winter solstice thus bringing to Moline boiling heat or freezing cold and every other type of climate in between.

The land is the same. Its deep, dark, rich soil full of nutrients will still raise the tallest corn and the tastiest tomatoes. The sun, the river, and the climate are still the same! Only some buildings and some builders have aged. Yet, this is true not only in my Moline, but in all places in all times. Just as most cities with their straight grids of streets and avenues once replaced quaint villages with rambling paths, so too, my Moline with its fine downtown district must now give way to its dispersal among many shopping centers.

Moline must also join the trend toward the megalopolis which is surely embracing it. When I was young we heard first about the twin cities and then about the tri-cities. Recently, I saw commercial signs proclaiming the quad cities and the quint cities. There were no sex cities, but I suppose this was more an attempt to dodge misinterpretation than anything else. In a recent map count of towns and cities that are contiguous to each other and eventually to Moline, I counted about a dozen different municipalities.

Surely, then, all can claim that you can find everything in Moline, because for its residents it still remains the center of the world!

Last picture of Mother and Ynez Bargas, 1977

EPILOGUE

I have written the story of some of my own and my family's experiences in finally finding a home in Moline, Illinois. In the process of doing enough research to ensure that the facts I've presented are as accurate as I can make them, I have become increasingly aware that my story and the story of my family can be duplicated by many other persons whose families came to Moline prior to the year 1925. I have also come to realize why there have been so few books written about Moline.

Moline is not really a separate geographical entity except in the minds of its city planners and politically appointed officials. Only the Mississippi River traces an easily definable border for this city. Moline is really but a segment of a growing orange. It cannot be dissected alive from the larger community of many names. It is inter-laced and inter-tied with lines of communication, roads of transportation, and bonds of association as numerous as the veins and arteries of any living being.

Moliners share this inter-dependent characteristic. They'll tell strangers what the old Moline High School fight song proclaims:

WE ARE MOLINERS,
WE'RE FROM MOLINE.
OUR TEAM'S THE FINEST
YOU'VE EVER SEEN.

The truth was told by John Donne as he wrote, "No man is an

island, entire of itself." Similarly, mankind and his cities, like all other forms of life, have been the product of all the factors that touched their lives. The individual is always just a microcosm of the forces that nurture him.

Probably, there are a lot of other Moliners who, like myself, take pride and pleasure in thanking the many good persons that helped us achieve our dreams. Moline just happened to be the place where I grew from a young illegal Mexican immigrant into a mature, proud, and happy American.

I feel certain that what happened to me in Moline was happening to a lot of other individuals like myself throughout the State of Illinois, and perhaps in a lot of other areas throughout the United States. Just as we had Mexican Dances and picnics in Moline, and similar functions in East Moline, Silvis, Rock Island, Bettendorf, Galesburg, Sterling, and so on, so too there were many other Mexican families growing, working, learning, and becoming important members of hundreds of other communities throughout the entire Midwest, and probably of all other areas of this country.

Since this integration was quiet and unobtrusive, little attention has been paid to this phenomenon. The simple act of perusing any telephone book will clearly show that the so-called Spanish-surnamed, especially from Mexico, have long been an integral part of the American scene.

ADDENDUM

Editor's Note: Shortly after the death of John Cervantes in 2009, several typewritten pages were discovered among his possessions. It is unclear exactly when these were written, but they serve to add some additional color to his story.

MY COUNTRY

My country is here! I don't really remember what Dad and Mother called "Mi Patria." I just remember that before we came here, my mother was very sad. Almost every single night, I could hear her cry after she put me into bed. But I think she cried because she missed my dad.

He was away in El Norte, earning money which he sent home so that we could buy food. He was away for a long, long time, and when my grandfather and my aunts would visit us in our little house in La Escoba, they would pick me up and say that I was "the little man of the house."

That made me feel very good, and even though I wasn't quite five years old, I decided to do everything I could to make Mother happy. So every day, I would go outside to see if I could find some ripe tunas, some wood, or a wildflower that I could bring to her. No matter what I found, she seemed glad to get it. She would hug me tight and call me "Mi Hijo," but after she put me to bed at night, I knew she was still sad. I could hear her sob softly.

I didn't know if I should go to comfort her, or if I should stay in bed and pretend that I was sleeping. One night, I got up and went to her, but I didn't know what to say. I just smoothed her hair and when she saw me standing near her, she cried out loud, hugged me, picked me up, and took me back to bed.

It always took me a long time to fall asleep, and even the days were very long for me. I was glad when mother sent me to grandfather's house to get milk and see if there was any mail for us. My mother's father was Pedro Ramos, and he lived on his small farm with my grandmother and their four daughters.

I used to think that my grandfather's house was far away, but mother could watch me nearly all the way, and my grandmother could see me as I came close to her house. She nearly always had something special for me to eat or to take back home.

Sometimes there was a letter from my dad with a money order inside. Then mother would read the letter over and over, again and again. If Dad wrote anything about me, she would read that part aloud, but mostly she read it to herself, and I think most of the time these letters made her more sad than happy, except the very last one.

That last letter made mother so happy that she jumped high into the air as she exclaimed, "He's coming home! He's coming home! Your daddy is coming home, and we'll never let him leave us again. Even if we starve! Whatever happens, we must stay together." There was no crying that night, nor the next night, nor the next night, nor ever again that I can remember.

Maybe I was the only one who was not overjoyed. Actually, I was a little bit worried. Of course I was glad that mother was so happy, but it had been a long time since I had seen my father, and I wondered whether he still liked me. I worried that I would not know what to say to him or how I should behave. Maybe when the big man of the house came home, there would no longer be a need for the little man of the house.

My worry was all for nothing. The afternoon he came home, there were so many other people with him, that I thought surely I would be lost in all the noise, loud talking, back slapping, hand-shaking, hugging, and kissing that was going on among my grandparents, aunts, uncles, cousins, other relatives, and friends who came to bring my dad home. I thought this big party would allow me to hide away in the farthest corner of the house, but then I heard my dad shout out in his loudest voice, "Where's my big boy?"

That made me so proud! Without thinking, I ran to him with my arms wide open, and as he picked me up to show me off to all of the rest, I asked myself, "Who wants to be the little man of the house when I already am my dad's big boy?"

REVOLUTION

Late that evening, after all the people had gone home, leaving Dad, Mother, and my baby brother Thomas by ourselves, I learned that we had been very lucky to have Dad come home. Only my Dad's father, Vicente Cervantes, had gone to the train station to meet my dad, and as they walked happily toward our house, they were suddenly overtaken by a large group of men on horseback that carried rifles, revolvers, and machetes. Immediately, as they were surrounded by the horsemen, a man who appeared to be the leader asked my dad in a very loud and angry voice, "Where did you get those boots?"

"I bought them in the United States," my dad answered softly.

"Do you expect us to believe you, when we know that those are government boots? Either you are a Federal soldier, or a thief. It doesn't make any difference to us which of these is true, because we are going to kill you anyway."

"My son is telling the truth," said my grandfather, and he added, "I just met him at the station. He doesn't take sides either with any of the revolutionaries or with the federals. All he wants to do is go home to his wife and family."

"Are you telling us that he is too big a coward to take sides in the fight for the life of his country?"

"I am telling you that he has been out of the country trying to earn enough money to feed his family. If you want his boots, he will give them to you."

"We don't need to ask either one of you for anything. Actually, we can take his boots and anything else we want before or after we kill him, and if you don't want us to kill you right now, you better leave and don't let us ever see you again."

He pointed a long, black revolver at him, pulled the hammer back with a loud click and hollered, "Now, go!"

As he said this, he threw a rope over Dad's head, and the whole group kicked up clouds of dust as they rode toward La Piedad with My dad running as fast as he could to try to keep up with their horses.

My grandfather, whom we called Papa Chente, said that when he was forced to leave the group, he climbed over one of the high, long rock fences that separate the fields and roads. Then he drew his pocket knife, and followed them, crouching low so the horsemen could not see him. He planned that if these men ever really tried to kill my dad, he would jump back over the fence and make sure to defend him with his own life.

Papa Chente was able to keep the group in sight without being discovered by them until they entered the main square of La Piedad. Here he was horrified to find that the whole center of town had been taken over by the revolutionaries, and that they had already stacked up many bodies of victims they had killed. It appeared that my dad would be next when my grandfather saw his brother Vidal among the civic leaders that had been forced to be there as witnesses. The killers were trying to justify their murders by falsely accusing their victims of interfering with the revolution.

"Vidal!" my grandfather shouted and pointed. "See my son Octaviano? Surely, you're not going to let him be killed!"

"You can bet our lives on that, Vicente," he yelled back as both of them stepped up to the leader, and after a loud, but short conversation, grandfather and his brother took my dad away and brought him home.

Every time I think about this terrible thing that nearly took my dad away from us, I become more frightened, even today, because I am sure that it was many times worse for him and for my grandfather. Still, there is one thing for which Mother might be thankful. She didn't have to convince my dad that we should stay together.

Late that night when they were talking of all the things that had happened, I heard my dad say very clearly, "We can not stay here any longer. We must leave this country and go where it will be safe to raise our children."

That made me very happy, and I quickly fell into a deep and peaceful sleep.

LA FRONTERA

At first, I thought our leaving would be quick and easy. That's because I didn't realize how many things had to be done first. Mother and Dad counted their money, and it was clear that they didn't have quite enough for our train tickets, even though they would not have to pay for me or for Tom.

Mother said they would have to sell the little cow that her father had given her, and which had been giving us the milk that I brought home each day. It made me sad to lose that pretty cow which I called "La Vaquita," but I knew we could not take her on the train.

The next decision was about what we should take with us. Mother wanted to take everything.

"Look, Octaviano," she said. "We have to take all of our clothes, my good dishes, and all of my pots and pans."

"And how are you going to carry all that stuff? Your hands will be full day and night just because you'll have to carry Tom all the time. He's only a year old."

"I know how old he is, and I think I can carry him and the bag with all our clothes, too. Vigen can carry a few light things."

Everybody called me Vigen, short for Edubigen, which is the name that was given to me when I was baptized.

"I can carry a lot," I interrupted. "At least, I can carry mama's good dishes."

"No," Dad said. "We'll wear our best clothes on the train, and take just one change of clothes with us in one bag. We'll also take one big metal pot and two tin cups that will fit inside the pot.

Vigen can carry that, but your mother will have to leave all of her dishes with your aunt Julia. Maybe someday we can come back for them and everything else that your Papa Pedro is willing to keep for us."

So, that's what we did as we waited for the train on a cool, bright morning. We saw its smoke first way off in the distance. It was black and curled high into the sky until it melted away into the blue. Next we heard its loud toot, toot, followed by the clanging of its swinging big bell. The closer the train came, the more uncertain I became. As the big, black giant of its engine swished past us like an angry bull, I could see and feel the clouds of steam rush by our faces, and I began to fear the huge power of this beast as it pulled about 10 coaches behind it.

Finally, it stopped, and a uniformed man with a black cap opened the door of one of the coaches and put down a little metal stool which all of us used as a step into an old red coach with seats and back rests made of wooden slats. Each back rest had a brass handle on top which was kept shiny by all the hands that held on to it whenever the passengers walked down the aisle as the train bounced and jumped, bumping along on its uneven tracks.

We had filled the pot with beans, and had carried a large cloth napkin into which Mama had tied about a dozen tortillas and six or eight tacos filled with meat, cheese and salsa. These really tasted good. After our food was gone, Dad would get off the train and buy food from vendors who walked around on the outside of the train, but none of that food tasted as good as our own.

I hated to see Dad leave the train, for fear that he would not get back on in time, and that the train would go on without him. At the end of our coach there was a little tank with water. It had a little button that you could press as you held a cup below the spout and out would drip the water we drank whenever we were thirsty.

It also had a very small bad smelling toilet in which I could barely fit, but all of us had to use it because the trip from our home to the border of the United States lasted almost three days. I felt particularly sorry for Mama because she had to carry my little brother day and night, resting only when Dad would take him for a while. She even slept with him in her arms.

I quickly got tired of the train ride. The seats were hard, and there was nothing to do. I took turns going to get a drink, going to the toilet, looking out of the window, or walking up and down the aisle. At first, there were a few children of different ages on the train. Some of the passengers even carried small animals such as rabbits and chickens, but as we got closer and closer to La Frontera we became the only family with children. Most of the other passengers were men with just a few women that seemed to be much older than my mother.

By that time, all of the passengers were talking about how they were going to cross the border. I listened so carefully that one of the few ladies finally took notice of my interest and asked where I was going by saying in Spanish, "A donde vas, niño?"

"A mi nueva patria," I replied.

"Ay, qué listo es este niño!" she said to her neighbor.

But, I didn't feel particularly smart. I wondered whether this "Frontera" was a big tall fence we would all have to climb over, or whether it might have a small door through which we would have to pass one at a time. In that case, I would have to make sure that I would not become separated from my mother. Tom was lucky because he and Mother would have to go through or over at the same time.

When I went back to our seats, Dad and Mother were discussing how they should get through that border. Dad told mother that it would be best if we went through customs as legal immigrants, but mother wasn't sure what they would make you do, nor whether they might let some of us through and keep others from crossing.

"No, they will not separate the families," my dad assured her. "They just want to check people who may be criminals, soldiers, or any one that has a communicable disease."

"Will they keep me and Vigen back? You know we both have these terrible colds from sleeping on these cold drafty coaches."

"I don't think so."

"Well, I don't want to take a chance if there is any other way. I don't ever want us to be separated again."

"When the train stops, we can just walk up to the bridge that separates Mexico from the United States, then we can go down to the river and pay someone on a boat to row us across. That's really not legal, but the worse thing they can do is to send us back here to Mexico."

"Well, then, we have very little to lose. So, let's do that."

My dad would sometimes disagree with my mother, but it seemed to me that she always won. She won again this time, and that's how I came to mi nueva patria. We all got into a large row-boat, and it only took about 10 minutes to cross the slow moving stream that was yellow and brown from all the mud it carried.

MY NEW NAME

Even before we landed on American soil, we could see that there were several wagons that seemed to be waiting. Each of these wagons had a team of horses all hitched up with a driver who bent over forward and seemed ready to go. Most wagons had another man sitting by the driver. As soon as we got on land, one of the wagons came right up to us. It was pulled by a team of horses that snorted, pawed the ground, and made the wagon creak as they tossed their manes and clink-clanked their harness as if they were impatient with waiting.

The driver pulled back on the reins shouting, "Whoa there, whoa Nellie, whoa Nicky."

As the horses quieted down, the man sitting next to the driver spoke to my dad in Spanish, "Are you looking for work?"

"Yes," my dad answered, and he turned toward Mama and he explained that he thought this was an "enganche."

"What's that?" Mama asked him just barely loud enough for me to hear.

"I represent the K.T. Railroad, and I can offer you an enganche if you've had experience as a section worker," the man said.

My dad quickly replied, "I've had more than two years' experience, but before I agree to go with you, I want to know exactly what this enganche includes. The most important thing is that I must have housing for my family."

"Well," the man said, "This is your lucky day. Not only do we guarantee you housing, but we will provide you with free transportation from here to the job, and you'll also get free food until you begin to work for us. Then, you can have credit at the nearest grocery store for as long as you continue to work for the K.T. Line."

"How's that sound to you, Lupe?" Dad asked my mother.

"Sounds too good to be true. So let's take it," she said.

Much later I learned that "enganche" in English means a hook, a snare, or to hire labor with false promises. This man's promises all turned out to be true. Dad was even transferred several times by the railroad company simply because he did not like the job, the boss, or his coworkers. We always had free transportation and free food between these jobs.

Finally, Dad quit the railroad so we could join my grandfather, Papa Chente, his two children, and my Aunt Concha and her five children. My aunt's husband, Martin Mendoza had died, and it was up to my dad, my grandfather, and my aunt to find some way to feed, clothe, and house all of us. We lived for a short time on the outskirts of Amarillo, Texas, and it was there that I started to go to school.

As long as we lived far from town in housing provided by the railroad for section workers, nobody really thought about school. However, as soon as we moved into Amarillo, my dad and mother realized that I had to go to school, or there was a very good chance that the Immigration Service would send us back to Mexico for violating the state's rules about compulsory school attendance. Furthermore, I was already seven years old, and it seemed clear that just for my own good, I needed to go to school like all the rest of the children.

Mother took me for my first day of school. It must have been about ten o'clock when we got to the four-story dark red brick building, and I wondered why there didn't seem to be anyone around. I was to learn that school started at 8:00 a.m., and that all of the students were in class when Mother and I arrived.

Somehow, she must have had me registered, and in no time at all, she took me into a room where the boys and girls were about my age and all of them seemed to be busy reading their books. The teacher was standing in front of the room, and she also had a book in her hand. Mother stepped up to where she was standing, handed her my registration, and then she turned around and left me standing in front of the class.

I had never felt so alone and abandoned. How could mother do this to me? Suddenly, I felt like running after her, but I knew that she would just bring me back. Next I thought about crying, but I was too big for that. Furthermore, all the children had stopped reading, and everyone was looking at me. So, I just stood there as straight as I could stand and looked at the teacher.

She seemed to be looking around the room. Finally, she turned to me, pointed her finger down one of the rows, and said something like, "Sit down there."

I said, "Dispénseme, pero no comprendo."

As soon as I said that I knew that neither one of us understood the other, and she must have thought exactly the same thing. She took me by the hand, led me down the row to an empty seat and repeated, "Sit down there." As she said this she pushed me down gently but firmly into the seat.

"Of course," I thought. She means, "Siéntese allí." So, for the rest of that class period I kept repeating to myself, "Sit down there! Sit down there! Sit down there!"

Before I knew it, a loud bell rang in my ear, and all the children got up, went into a little hallway, took some paper bags and lunch pails, and went out to the yard. I was the last to leave. I had expected to be directed to do something, but when the teacher took her own paper bag out of her desk drawer and walked out of the room, I got up and walked after her.

The school yard was like a giant ant hill. All the children continued to pour out of one main doorway, and as soon as they were out on the blacktop, they went into different directions, as if they each had a special thing to do. Some went to sit in the shade to eat whatever they had brought for lunch, others began throwing and catching different balls. Some of the girls sat on the steps to play jacks, while a few boys drew large circles on the ground and started to shoot marbles. It seemed to me that I was the only one with nothing to do, so I just stood against the building and watched.

I would have been happy to spend the rest of the day just watching, but very soon I was drawn into a game that I neither understood nor appreciated. Two boys who were about my size came and stood in front of me and one seemed to ask, What's your name?"

I looked first at him and then at the other. Then I shook my head to indicate that I didn't understand. Then the other spoke louder than the first one, but he seemed to ask the same question, "What's your name?"

I became very uncomfortable because I didn't know what to do. They just kept taking turns asking, "What's your name?"

"What's your name?"

As I stood with my back to the wall wondering whether I should run away and find some place to hide, a bigger boy came and stood next to me as if to join me, and looking first at me and then at the other boys said, "Tell them, 'Pudding Tame, and if you ask me again, I'll tell you the same.'"

This seemed to discourage the other two, particularly when he repeated, "Tell them, 'Pudding Tame, and if you ask me again, I'll tell you the same.'"

Suddenly a loud bell rang, and nearly everybody began to make a line to go back into the school. Two girls who had been playing jacks picked up their ball and jacks, put them into a little cloth bag, but instead of walking back toward the school's entrance, they came up to where I was still backed up against the wall.

"Let him alone," one said as she took me by the hand. "His name is — Jack."

As to welcome and thank them for their friendship I nodded my head and repeated, "Jack."

Then the group broke up and we all got into the line of boys and girls that were walking back into school. When I got back into my seat the teacher gave me some books, paper, and a pencil. Then she went back to teaching the class. I tried my best to follow what she was saying, but I couldn't understand her at all. The best I could do, was to notice what the other boys and girls around me were doing, and I tried my best to do the same. The only thing that stuck into my mind was the incident during the lunch period and the name "Jack." It seemed to have some kind of magic!

On the way home, the same two girls who had rescued me at noon waited for me after school and walked me home. On the way, one would keep asking, "What's your name?" And the other would simply reply, "Jack," then she pointed to me. Eventually I began to repeat the word, "Jack," after the question, "What's your name?" That became my first lesson in English, and the name Jack stuck with me for the rest of my life!

MONTANA

I only went to school in Amarillo for a about a month. My grandfather, my dad, and my Aunt Concha decided to take an enganche to the sugar beet fields of Montana. There we would all be living on a farm again, and most of us would be able to help with the work the farmer wanted us to do. Again, we were promised free transportation, food, and housing. This time there would be 13 of us travelling, living, and working together on one beet field.

Once more we rode the train. Somehow, this trip didn't seem too long. We had a lot of fun because there were so many of us, and we were all family. My grandfather was a widower, and he had two children, my Aunt Jesse and my Uncle Joe. He was only a year older than I. My Aunt Concha's husband had died recently, and she was left with my cousins; Marcella, Hilda, Rosie, Ruby, and Martin, Jr. He was just a little baby. My dad and mother had also added to the family. Now besides me and my brother Tom, we also had another baby named Leonard. We had adopted these English names instead of our Spanish names, because we thought they would be easier for the Americans to pronounce.

On the third day of our train trip, we arrived in Billings, Montana. Here we were met at the station by the farmer we were supposed to work for. He had brought a big wagon which was drawn by a team of four horses. Later, I learned that this wagon was used for hauling sugar beets. The side boards were taller than any of the adults. At the signal from the farmer, we climbed into the wagon with all of our belongings. There was still plenty of room for us children to run around and play a little game of tag. Soon, our parents made us stop for fear that we might fall off the rear of the wagon which only had a short tailgate.

That made our wagon trip seem longer, but we quietly tried to count the clop-clop of the horses' hooves, and the clink-clanking and squeaking of their harness. The sun was setting like a giant ball of flaming fire, and its red, orange, and purple colors seemed to bathe the whole western sky when we finally reached our field in Huntley, Montana.

When we got off the wagon, the farmer took us to two houses. The one nearest the road was the larger one. My grandfather and my Aunt Concha took that one for themselves and for their children. There was a smaller house in the back of the larger one. My dad and mother took it for the rest of us.

When we had unloaded our things and put them into the houses where we were going to stay, the farmer made it clear that only the adults could work in the fields, and that the children would have to go to school in the fall. It was now late in June, the beginning of summer vacation. I had become used to school in Amarillo. I wondered what it would be like here in Montana, but what interested me most at this time was the wide, deep ditch that ran in back of our houses. I could barely wait to go dip my feet in that clear, fast running stream.

That ditch became our own private swimming pool. The days seemed to be longer and hotter here than anywhere I had been before. Everybody got up at sunrise, and after a hurried breakfast, all of us would go into the fields. My cousin Hilda and I did not have to work. Our parents would try to find some shady spot where we could stay and watch the children that were younger than we were. I was stuck with my brother Tom and our baby Leonard. Hilda had to watch her sisters Rosie and Ruby and baby Martin. The rest of the family went to work on the endless rows of sugar beets.

It seemed like forever before they got to the end of the long, long rows. Finally, they would turn around to work different rows, and eventually they would return to where they had left us. Now, they would spend a little time talking to us and making us as comfortable as possible. At noon, we would all sit together and share the lunches they had packed, but we never got started back home until the long shadows of evening told us that darkness would be coming soon.

Homecoming was the best time of all! Everyone that wanted to do so would jump into the ditch in their underwear to cool off and to wash off the dust of the fields.

My grandfather and my Aunt Concha never joined the bathers. They carried water from the ditch in pails, warmed it on the stove, then poured the water into a big wash tub. Then each would take turns enjoying a warm bath.

That ditch was where we got all of our water, including the water for cooking and for drinking. Each evening, my Aunt Concha would come to where we were playing in the ditch to see if we were all safe, and to get some water to use in the house. Usually she carried two big pails and came in a big hurry. One evening, my cousin Hilda and I began playing on the bank, and without thinking much about it we started to throw water onto the bank.

We kept doing this, until we got the idea of sliding down the dripping bank into the water to make a big splash. We were taking turns on our water slide, when my aunt came running down to fill her pails. We knew she was in a hurry to make supper, so Hilda and I moved aside as she stepped into the middle of our slide and made the biggest splash of the evening. Hurriedly, we rescued the pails and took some water into the house where my grandfather was waiting impatiently for his supper.

"Where's Concha?" he roared.

I answered, "She's taking a bath."

"What's the matter with her? Has she gone crazy?"

EDITOR'S AFTERWORD

My grandfather John Cervantes first published *My Moline* in 1986. It was the culmination of many years of research and writing. Although it has been nearly nine years since his death in 2009, his memory lives on with his family and the scholarship that bears his name.

This book, however, has been completely out of print for 20-plus years, until now. This revised edition corrects several factual and typographical errors from the original work. And the typography has been redesigned in a more modern style.

Some photographs from the original have been omitted, in favor of other photographs and newspaper clippings that have been found since the original printing. Many of the photographs retained here from the original have been placed in more appropriate locations in the book. Aside from these changes, the work has largely been unchanged. The chaptering is still the same, and the story still reads as originally intended.

My gratitude goes to all who helped me update my grandfather's work, including my father Jim Atkinson, who provided a digital version of the original book and digitized many of Mr. C.'s old photographs; my mother Mary Atkinson, who counseled me on numerous matters and helped me gather photos; my uncle Paul Cervantes, who provided digital versions of several of the photographs; my mother's cousins Marylou Witherspoon and Pam Clemens, who tracked down some long lost family photos in the Quad Cities with help from my great-aunt Margaret Lopez.

In addition, my aunt Elizabeth Cervantes Kukla discovered and mailed to me the separate typewritten pages that I've included in the preceding Addendum section of this book.

Thank you also to Emma Lincoln, special collections librarian at Augustana College's Thomas Tredway Library, for her assistance in helping me obtain the photograph of downtown Moline used on the cover of this edition.

For more information about *My Moline*, additional supplementary materials, and an interactive map of key places, please visit JohnCervantes.org.

Jimmy Atkinson
October 17, 2017